Balanced:
The Al Pearlstein Story

By Mark Pearlstein

2017

First Printing: 2017

ISBN-13: 978-1544075617
ISBN-10: 1544075618

DISCLAIMER

CONTENTS

ACKNOWLEDGMENTS

Someone once said that the ancestor of every action is a thought. But in making my book a reality, the practicalities of this process turned the experience into an extended relay race. I could not have completed it without much support, understanding and expertise from teams of people, each passing the baton through to the finish line. I am truly grateful to those who helped me on my incredible journey of recording my family's roots, Al's story and his legacy of learning, doing and helping others. They include:

My family and friends for encouraging, listening, remembering, being interviewed, reviewing and consulting:

- Sharon, my wonderful wife, and my children, Daniel, Samara and Zachary;
- Al and Beth, my parents, whose love and values have inspired me in so many ways;
- Debbie, Geoff and Melissa, my siblings, who provided valuable feedback;
- Gloria Houser, Eddie Sheffman, Marlene Matlow and Gloria Fischbach, all close relatives whose insights added so much colour to my stories;
- Dr. Wayne R. Samsoondar, our resident health and wellness expert;
- Robin Altman, founder of Radiate Coaching, who helped me build a platform of purpose, creativity and innovation; and
- Merle Kastner, Vice-President and Program Chair, Jewish Genealogy Society of Montreal, whose shared passions of family and history were indispensable.

Al's colleagues, who graciously gave their time to be interviewed:

- Brian Ayer, retired Branch Manager, RBC Dominion Securities;
- John W. Braive, Vice-Chairman, CIBC Global Asset Management Inc.;
- John D. Cannell, retired Chief Operating Officer, Pension Fund Society, Toronto Transit Commission;
- Robert Goldberg, Investment Advisor, Caldwell Securities;

- John Markle, Trustee, Metropolitan Toronto Pension Plan;
- Joan Marshall, retired Vice-President and Chief Compliance Officer, RBC Dominion Securities;
- Ward C. Pitfield, founder of Pitfield, Mackay Ross Limited, 1967-1984;

My team at RBC Dominion Securities who did all the countless things that needed to be done behind the scenes as the book was being compiled including photographing half the images that help tell the story:

- Katrina Mijares, Associate;
- Sam Kim, Associate Advisor and Financial Planner.

My exceptionally skilled book publishing team, with whom I consulted on writing, copy editing and self-publishing:

- John Lorinc, Angela Misri and Joyce Grant.

My innovative creative team for designing a brilliant cover that captures the essence of the book:

- Simon Burn, SDB Creative Group Inc.;
- Andy Strote, Integrated Marketing entrepreneur;
- Bret Teskey, Owner/Photographer, Modern Imagery Photography Studio.

Preface: Five Days in Berlin

I decided to write this book while flying back home from Berlin over the Canada Day long weekend in 2012. My brother Geoff, brother-in-law Norm and I had taken my dad Al, to see Berlin as an undivided city for his eighty-fifth birthday. Al always had a special place in his heart for learning and history. As he has told me many times, if my grandfather Harry, at age 23, hadn't left Lithuania in 1925 for North America, the chances were good that our family would have perished in Hitler's rise to power.

When I told my friends and family members what we were doing, I received varied responses. "Why there?" some asked. Others wondered if we would feel strange making such a journey. I had traveled to Germany before, and from an historical perspective, Al wanted to go. So, we went.

While there, we visited the Brandenburg Gate, the Bundestag (the restored German parliament building), and the Olympiastadion, the site of the infamous 1936 Olympics. For Al, they were all incredibly interesting places.

But there was one story in particular that played out in front of the old German army headquarters, now a museum. This is what gave me the inspiration to somehow weave the past, present and future into a book.

Our guide was Thorsten Wagner, a 40-something, 6'6" giant of a man and a Danish university professor of Jewish Studies. On a gorgeous June day, as he explained the significance of this museum to our small group, Al blurted out a single phrase: "July 20, 1944." Thorsten couldn't believe Al had not only mentioned that day, but had also anticipated its significance on our tour. That was the date when senior German army officers had tried unsuccessfully to assassinate Adolf Hitler, in order to shorten his horrific war. It was in the courtyard of this museum that the key plotters had been shot.

Then Al asked Thorsten if he knew how Hitler had financed the war. After Thorsten admitted that money wasn't his strong suit, Al explained that a German banker, Hjalmar Horace Greeley Schacht, who had served as Hitler's minister of economics, had been the mastermind.

Where did Schacht get his strange name? Once again, Al knew the story. He explained that Schacht's father left Germany for the U.S. after the American Civil War, in search of a better life. Schacht Sr. couldn't make a go of it, and moved back to Germany. But during his stay in the U.S., he had developed a love for Horace Greeley, the well-known American journalist who coined the phrase, "Go west, young man." Needless to say, Thorsten and my dad hit it off.

Thorsten said he had never met anyone quite like Al before. He found Al's grasp of history simply astonishing. It didn't matter where we went, my dad had something to teach us all, in his understated way.

In fact, Al has always sought to not only absorb historical knowledge, but to learn deeply from it and make those narratives come alive. He frequently shared insights and perspectives while helping his family and many others throughout his long and illustrious career in the Toronto investment community.

It was during the flight back from Berlin that I started writing about that visit and thinking about how I could connect the stories of my grandfather, my father and myself. My grandfather, Harry, went west from Lithuania to Newfoundland. My father continued from St. John's to Los Angeles but returned to Toronto.

Looking back, one link between their journeys is that they made life-changing decisions in their early to mid-20s, as did I.

All three of my siblings and I are very fortunate to live and work in Toronto. We don't have to travel far to be with family and to celebrate life, thanks to my father and his father, both of whom did much of the heavy lifting for us.

Three generations encompass many different cycles, both in life and investing. As I consider that longer perspective, I'm struck by even more questions that I had been yearning to have answers for since I was a child. Where did my interest in understanding the way the world worked come from? Was it nature or nurture? How was I going to take these thoughts and find a purpose for them? How can I serve others by adapting what I have learned from Al to help people manage their money and wealth?

In the process of conducting the research for this book, journaling and writing and interviewing my parents, I found answers. By spending the time to get my father's story down on paper, I discovered things I never knew before, about him and about myself. I didn't expect that, but I'm grateful that I can share what I've learned with my family, my friends and my clients. The pivots for me were to stop and think, to look back for context and then to look forward to experience life's journey.

Introduction: The Den

In 1955, my parents, Al and Beth Pearlstein, bought their first home—a comfortable split-level house in a newly developed model suburb known as Don Mills, situated on Toronto's northeast fringe. They paid $19,500 and did the deal with a man named Al Latner, who went on to become one of the city's preeminent builders.

At the time, Al and Beth were living in a five-storey red-brick apartment building on Bathurst Street near Eglinton Avenue. But they had reached a stage in their lives when they were ready to move up. Though not yet 30, Al had already established a flourishing career as a stockbroker, initially for Milner, Ross & Co. and then with Ross, Knowles & Co. My elder sister, Debbie, had just arrived. And my mother, trained as a nurse at St. Michael's Hospital, had decided to stay home and raise the baby.

As they surveyed the booming city, my parents briefly considered moving to an older residential neighbourhood just a few blocks north of their apartment, but instead decided to take a risk on one of the subdivisions that had sprung up from the languid pastures and sprawling estates that stretched out along the Don Valley.

With its cul de sacs, modern schools and lush parks, the area seemed like the next frontier but Al's reasons were, as ever, informed by a strong sense of the practical.

"I was driving downtown to Queen and Bay and I realized the traffic wasn't getting any better," he said. "But then I found out that the Don Valley Parkway was going to be built, so I thought the work commute would be better if we moved to Don Mills." As my mother used to say, the giant water tower on the east side of Leslie Street was our landmark.

Geoff, Debbie and me playing, 1963, with the Don Mills water tower, our landmark, in the background.

By the fall of 1963, my parents were presiding over a bustling young family that had grown to include my elder brother Geoff and myself; my younger sister Melissa was on the way. Having outgrown that first Don Mills tract house, they decided to trade up to a larger one not far away, in an enclave developed on a former golf course. I was almost five at the time and distinctly remember my mother crying over the news of President John F. Kennedy's assassination.

We moved to the new house, at 58 Foursome Cres., the following spring. It was a tidy dwelling made from pale ochre bricks, with a two-car garage out front and five bedrooms upstairs. The wide sash windows, framed by dark brown shutters, overlooked a broad driveway. The dining room and the kitchen looked out over the backyard.

Growing up, our family enjoyed a comfortable, middle-class lifestyle.

Like most of my friends, I played a lot of ice and road hockey, and watched hockey, football and movies on the console television in the basement. An ice cream truck often appeared on warm evenings.

My mother, ever thrifty, would never give us money, even though we always asked. Once, my brother and I worked ourselves into such histrionics about not being allowed to buy ice cream that we ran directly into one another. I had a black eye, and there was lots of crying, but my mother didn't give an inch. Al had taught her well.

My parents didn't own a cottage; instead, we spent our free time at the Donalda Club, a scenic 200-acre golf and country club located in a nearby ravine. It offered golf, tennis, swimming and other activities, including family meals in the informal dining room.

When I think back on my childhood, however, I find myself drawn to one particular space—Al's den, which opened off the foyer on the main floor, with its curtained windows looking out over the front garden.

Me, left, with Debbie and Geoff, with Melissa as a baby, in the den, mid-1964.

The den was hardly a man cave by contemporary standards. Al had furnished it with a hard, uncomfortable couch near the door. The décor included a barometer and two toddler portraits of my brother and me dressed up in sailor suits, as well as family photos of my mother and two sisters. The wall covering was a spongy cork, a popular material at the time.

The room's most conspicuous and dominant feature, was the built-in bookshelf that extended the entire length of the wall opposite the windows. Below shelves laden with stern looking volumes, there was a long Arborite countertop with cupboards at both ends and a workspace in the middle. This was Al's desk, a sacred place where he'd retreat after dinner to read, think and line up his schedule for the next day.

When I was a child, Al allowed me to come into his den in the evenings while he worked at his desk, but only on certain conditions: no toys and no noise. I passed the time flipping through the periodicals on the coffee table: *Time, Newsweek* and *U.S. News & World Report*. Despite the decidedly Spartan atmosphere and a lack of the typical childhood distractions, my dad's quiet company provided a very reassuring kind of warmth.

Yet Al's rules also subtly encouraged me to absorb the life lessons he has prized for as long as I can remember: read widely, be prepared and use your time wisely. He liked to tell anyone who'd listen that most people waste about six hours every day, and so he always took care to be as productive as possible, which meant thinking about the challenges and opportunities that confronted his clients every day. That's what he did in his den and it's what I learned from him at an early age.

As he sat at his desk, he read his business magazines and studied the books on investing, politics and world affairs that he would subsequently refer to friends and colleagues.

One title in particular stands out in my memory—a stout hardcover with a black spine and gold lettering: "Applied Imagination: Principles and Procedures of Creative Problem Solving, by Alex F. Osborn. It sat in the middle of his bookshelf, just above eye level, as if it was a keystone to a structure.

A former ad industry executive who co-founded BBDO, Osborn was the father of brainstorming, a term he not only coined, but turned into a national preoccupation by the mid-1950s. The 415-page treatise, published just two years after Norman Vincent Peale's "The Power of Positive Thinking," offered practical advice on how to unleash the imagination at a time when thought-leaders like Osborn were fretting about how Americans had grown slack due to the advent of labour-saving devices, consumer conveniences and habits of mind that discouraged audacity and ingenuity. "[I]maginative ability," Osborn said in his book, "can be improved through practice."

In the mid-1950s, Al had heard about "Applied Imagination" from a university friend, Burke Brown. My dad was enrolled in commerce and finance at the University of Toronto, while Burke studied psychology. What brought them together was an investment club Burke had set up called Cardinal Investments. As Al recalls, Burke had a knack for always coming up with new and different ideas.

Burke, at the time an early venture capitalist, loved looking into new types of businesses and the sorts of fresh approaches that come from entrepreneurs or inventors. Al found his friend's habit intriguing, especially since he had been in the investment business for only a few years. "Applied Imagination," Burke had told Al, offered practical advice on how to push oneself to generate questions and ideas, and move beyond the habitual self-censorship that can easily extinguish innovation.

I once asked Al why that book was situated where it was on his bookshelf in the den. He told me he'd long ago come to the conclusion that "Applied Imagination" was worth reading periodically, so he wanted it to be easily accessible. What, I wondered, did he mean by 'periodically'? Maybe once every three years or so? Al replied that he made a notation on his desk calendar to re-read the book every December—something he did for 20 years running.

To someone who doesn't know Al, that story may seem eccentric. But to me, and to those who've had the privilege of working with him or befriending him, the anecdote opens a window on a remarkably nimble and curious mind. Al reads widely. He is, in every way, a student of life—a person who has sought to understand the workings of the world. His determination is such that he also devoted a portion of his intellectual energy to thinking about thinking, which is, really, what Osborn encouraged in his book.

Al also valued these habits of mind in the people he wanted to have around him professionally. Co-workers and those in his professional circle repeatedly received recommendations on what to read and how to seek more knowledge.

Just as he keeps up a strict daily regimen of exercise to maintain his physical well-being, Al believes fervently in the importance of intellectual fitness and imparts this lesson to family, friends and colleagues. To this day, if he suggests that I read something that's crossed his radar, I follow his advice. I am rarely disappointed.

Robert Goldberg, a Toronto retail broker who worked at Burns Fry Ltd. for many years and was mentored by Al, recalls a moment in the 1970s, early in his career, when he decided to transition from trading commodities in a family company to the brokerage business. Goldberg knew Al because Al had been his father's broker since the early 1960s.

"'What do I need to do?'" Goldberg recalls asking Al when they met for lunch to discuss career prospects. "His answer was very simple and made sense: 'Read.' My next question was, 'Read what?' So he gave me a reading list."

It included everything from mainstream business magazines like *Forbes* and *Businessweek* to more eclectic titles such as "Extraordinary Popular Delusions and the Madness of Crowds," an 1841 account of history's most notorious investment bubbles and get-rich-quick schemes, by the Scottish journalist Charles Mackay.

Goldberg recounts that Al offered up other nuggets of wisdom, about how to avoid some of the negative afflictions a life on Bay Street could bring (e.g. alcoholism and family break-up). But his advice on why it's critical for investment advisors to situate learning at the very centre of the profession proved to be a key to sustainable success in a business that attracted aggressive and sometimes misleading sales tactics. In his career as a stockbroker and later as an advisor to pension plan investment boards, Al demonstrated a deep and holistic understanding of market cycles, the critical importance of interest rates and the fluid connections between macroeconomic forces, global or national politics and the decisions taken by investors, firms and the executives who guide them.

"He would say, 'You've got to know what you're trading,'" Goldberg says. He recalls listening intently on numerous occasions as Al would tease apart various factors that were influencing a company's decisions and actions. He would pick out the places where interests were aligning or in conflict, Goldberg remembers.

"He would start with, 'Did you see this article?' From there, he would devolve the entire construct behind that small reference.

"Al was very good at bringing all the factors one could collate and consolidate [what was] influential on key decision-makers. And from there, you had to make a choice: Was this investment good or bad? Were you going to be caught on- or offside?"

* * *

As we become mature adults and then have children of our own, most of us will eventually begin to think differently about our parents. We learn to see them less as guardians, providers, dispensers of praise or punishment or perhaps even adversaries, and more like ordinary human beings, each endowed with their own collections of gifts and failings. Where we once saw larger-than-life figures, we grow to understand their struggles and gain some perspective on the way they handled their duties as caregivers.

My parents provided my siblings and me with material comforts, structure and love. They worked hard, spent carefully, saved and invested in their family in every sense of that word. Beth taught us the value of a dollar and Al stressed, by his own example, the importance of treating everyone with respect and dignity.

As a consequence of my parents' effort and determination, I grew up in a comfortable, middle-class neighbourhood with good schools, initially dreaming about a hockey career and later finding my way into an MBA program and then banking, the profession that marked the first five years of my career.

All the while, my father continued to do his thing in his customary low-key way. For all his many successes—Al was, for years, one of the top stockbrokers on Bay Street and widely respected within his industry—he never boasted. In fact, despite his prowess as a wealth manager (long before that phrase existed) and then a pension plan consultant, he never pushed any of us to follow him into the investment world.

But when my brother Geoff and I decided to join his practice, in 1985 and 1990 respectively, we began to see why he had gained so many admirers. He took care to learn what his clients needed. Al's comprehensive due diligence helped him fully understand their goals and risk tolerances, which continues to be a regulatory focus today. Rather than spending time trading his own account or indulging in long liquid lunches, he researched meticulously, developing only a handful of key investment recommendations each year.

Based on his scholarship and experience, he used an aspirational asset allocation formula—the "fixed equity ratio," which called for a portfolio to include about 30% equities and 30% bonds, with the balance invested in response to market conditions and economic cycles—for his clients' portfolios, which he believed would blunt the impact of short-term market fluctuations and build value over the long term.

Throughout his career, he always took care to educate his clients about the ebb and flow of market cycles and dissuade them from trading stocks back and forth.[1]

---

[1]When meeting clients, Al explained his view on how the odds were stacked against short-term trading, based on a one-page handout he entitled, "Small Profits and Big Losses." He'd begin by saying that if he made 10 buy recommendations over a three-year period, not all would experience positive returns. Al liked to recommend stocks which he believed would increase in value 50 to 100 per cent in three years, although he always cautioned that there are no guarantees in the market. Still, Al believed it would be reasonable to assume that there will be three losers and limit the loss to 30 per cent on each. Moreover, he continued, the projection of a 100-per-cent gain is high, so he assumed a 50-per-cent gain. Now, say three stocks lose 30 per cent each, meaning the overall value drops by 90 per cent. Seven others, in turn, gain 50 per cent each, which adds 350 per cent. In other words, the net total gain over three years is 260 per cent, or an

As I came to realize, he laid that knowledge groundwork for a good reason: a market contrarian, Al firmly believed that the wise investor—which is to say the investor prepared to listen to the kind of dispassionate analysis that was Al's stock-in-trade—won't be blinded by greed or crippled by fear.

He always counselled his clients to be mindful of the cycle. Don't try to be the first in, and know when to lighten up and when to add. Most importantly, Al stressed the importance of taking the long view of wealth creation by drawing on an early philosophy of value investing which he would refer to as the fixed equity ratio.

While assessing clients' specific needs, he built portfolios based on his investment belief that they should include a minimum of 30 per cent in equity and 30 per cent in fixed income, with reserves to vary the mix for the remaining 40 per cent.

Al's clients listened, and many saw their retirement savings (and lifestyle options) experience fewer ups and downs as a consequence.

Al's world view, of course, infused the business I joined in 1990, and indeed still does, even though specific investment and asset allocation strategies have evolved in recent years with the introduction of so many new financial products.

This project has also grown from the process of learning how Al went about building wealth for his clients. In 2012, as Al, then age 85, finally slowed his pace (ever so slightly), I decided to

---

average of 26 per cent per stock over three years. That works out to eight per cent annually. Ultimately, the chances of being a successful trader are about one in five, and those odds decline over time. See: http://www.marketwatch.com/story/the-odds-of-day-trading-yourself-to-a-profit-are-lower-than-you-expect-2016-08-19 and https://faculty.haas.berkeley.edu/odean/papers/Day%20Traders/Day%20Trading%20and%20Learning%20110217.pdf.

begin interviewing him—about his childhood in Newfoundland and California, his career in Toronto and his accumulated wisdom about the way markets function. Through those discussions and further interviews with other family members, friends and colleagues, I developed an understanding of how growing up in Depression-era Newfoundland and Al's early health struggles not only shaped his outlook, but also instilled in him a firm belief in the importance of learning, a balanced lifestyle and the role of family.

Indeed, throughout his career, Al never lost sight of the interplay between our life choices, long-term investment strategies and goals. I began to absorb these lessons long ago, in the den in our house. Many decades later, Al's teaching continued to form the foundation of my philosophy of wealth management and also of my life outside the practice. Following his example, I sought out a life/work balance so my job never felt like work. I am able to take care of my family and myself, and my wife Sharon and I can spend time together travelling, watching our family grow or just hanging out in the backyard.

Me in front of my house, 1965; a year before my learnings began in my dad's den.

Finally, this book emerged from a period of deep personal reflection, as I sought to reinvent myself and my practice within the context of the rapidly changing field of wealth management.

To get there, I decided to draw on help from an executive coach and business consultant, and deliberately chose someone from outside the wealth management industry. It has turned out to be one of the best personal and business decisions I've ever made. This book grew from a creativity and innovation program I took with executive coach Robin Altman, who taught me about purpose, passion and serendipity and who offered her insights about how all the pieces fit together.

Part I: Al's Story

Chapter 1: Vištytis

In 2016, I decided to do some genealogical detective work to gather together the stories of Al's family tree, whose roots stretch back to the languid farm country in southwest Lithuania, near the Polish and German borders.

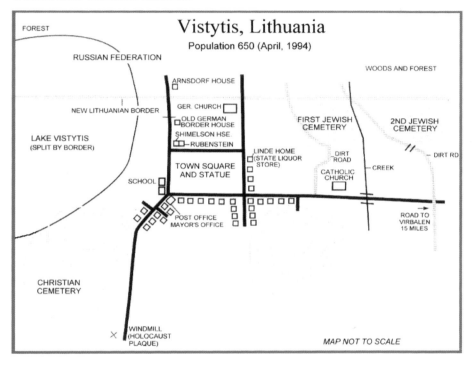

The town where my grandfather and great-grandfather were born. Source: Jewish Gen

Growing up, the past was always part of my present.

For as long as I can remember, Al, who read voraciously about history and politics, had talked about both world wars. He told me about the difference between labour camps and concentration camps, urged me to read important books like "One Day in the Life of Ivan Denisovich," by the Soviet dissident writer Aleksandr Solzhenitsyn, and made sure I learned Jewish history at Sunday school. In university, I studied these topics to complement my commerce courses and later my political science degree. One in particular stood out: an inspiring professor lectured about the unification of Germany in 1871 and the way that monumental event came to shape Europe through the first half of the 20th century. Amidst all the information I soaked up about the continent's bloody past, a key detail always stood out. Al's father, Harry, who lived near us until he died when I was 33, originally came from Vištytis, a hamlet that was sometimes in Germany and sometimes in Poland; its national borders kept moving as the political winds shifted. (The town, which is now in Lithuania, is also called Vishtinetz.) From my comfortable home in Canada, I wondered what it would have been like to live in such difficult and unstable circumstances. I wanted to know more about this ground zero and how Harry had survived, come to Canada and made a life for himself.

The 41-page document that emerged from my attempts to answer these questions is at once elegant and eclectic. It is a compendium that includes a complex family tree whose tendrils extend across the Atlantic, as well as contemporary group photos, memoirs, letters, reproductions of official documents and a few modest snapshots of the village where this journey begins, on a cattle farm a few kilometres from town.

I should say that I've never been to Vištytis, or Lithuania for that matter, although I hope to make that journey someday. But one of Al's cousins, Marlene Shapiro Matlow, made the journey in the fall of 1990, when the edifice of the Soviet Union was crumbling. Her moving letters home about that visit—reproduced in this book—offer me a revealing glimpse of a remote place that seemed to have been frozen in time for much of the Cold War.

Oct 29/90

My dear grand niece
Marlene & family.
It was very nice to hear from you with all the news about VISTINITZ, where your grandfather + I were born. Unfortunately I was only able to recognize a few of the pictures. I cannot recall the cemetery as pictured, but the church is familiar. I believe that it is 2 blocks from where we lived. also one street away was the road to Germany - about 1/4 of a mile away.

Letter indicating my grandfather had a home in the town.

Marlene, who lived in southern California, and Al, my father, were second cousins; her grandfather, Tanchem, and Al's father were brothers. A curious detail about that relationship is that both men went by the informal name Harry. Tanchem Pearlstein was born in Vištytis in 1880, the fourth of 10 brothers; Al's father, Harry, was born in the same village 22 years later, the tenth sibling.

According to Marlene's account, her group traveled initially to Vilnius. But Soviet-era tourism officials informed them that they wouldn't be allowed to journey to Vištytis, as it was located in a closed region. Undaunted, Marlene and her group found a guide and persuaded him to take them through the countryside in the direction of the family's ancestral home. After passing through a pastoral landscape dotted with farms, they came across a sign pointing toward Vištytis. "I was very emotionally happy," she wrote, adding that she was hopeful that she and her group would meet villagers who might not only remember the name Pearlstein, but point them to the farmhouse where their grandfather and grandmother had lived.

The town itself, she reported, was charming. Her guide made some inquiries as to who they should talk to about finding the old farm. They were directed to some of the older residents, but when the translator asked them about the Pearlstein homestead, all of them offered up the same answer: "The only Jewish people who were in Vištytis were shopkeepers. None of the Jewish people who lived here were rich enough to own 30 acres of land and cattle."

"I was," Marlene wrote, "very disappointed."

But when she and the guide proceeded to tour through the overgrown Jewish cemetery on the edge of the village, they discovered something that seemed to sharply contrast with the vague recollections of those elderly residents.

"This cemetery was filled with gravestones. Perhaps a thousand or thousands of them. The many years of growth made walking very difficult. It must have been a least a foot deep with undergrowth. The older stones were so old that the Hebrew etching had faded away … I felt sad and emotional because even if I could find my great-grandfather's grave, I'd be unable to know it because I can't read Hebrew. It was still a great feeling to be there because I knew and felt I had family in this cemetery."

* * *

In the middle of the 14th century, a deadly epidemic dubbed the Black Death wiped out much of the population of western Europe and triggered an exodus. According to the autobiography of Jacob Rubinstein, who was born in Vištytis in 1890, the Jews were blamed for the catastrophe. "Because Jews suffered less than the general population due to their hygienic laws in the matter of food preparation," he wrote in our history, "they were accused of poisoning the wells."

In the 1380s, many Jews who had lived in Germany and Poland began settling in the area now known as Lithuania, a lowland area on the southeast elbow of the Baltic Sea. But within a century, anti-Jewish agitation was again spreading across Europe, culminating in the expulsion of the Jews from Spain in

1492. Lithuania expelled its Jews in 1495.

Just eight years later, however, Alexander, the King of Poland and Archduke of Lithuania, changed his mind: "We have permitted them to dwell in all places in our estates and cities where they were formally to be found ... give them their House of Prayer and graveyard and likewise the farms and fields as before."[2]

In the coming decades, Jewish councils, semi-autonomous local government-like entities, won the right to lease and operate large swaths of land through an arrangement known as an arenda.[3] The council's managers could lease out mills, distilleries, fishponds, farms, inns, beehives and woodlots, often to Jewish families, in exchange for rent. Jewish councils also collected local taxes and levies on behalf of the central government. The Lithuanian-Polish Jews prospered because of the franchises, but their economic success triggered an all-too-familiar backlash; state officials tried (unsuccessfully) to cancel the leases in 1569. The antagonism continued to build. A wave of vicious attacks by Cossacks in 1648, coupled with the misery of a long-running regional war as well as harassment and blood libels, roiled Lithuania's Jewish community, forcing the councils to pay large bribes for protection.

In the late 18th century, the borders that had alternatively sheltered and exiled Lithuania's Jews shifted when Catherine the Great established the Pale of Settlement, a largely autonomous and predominantly Jewish region that straddled modern-day

---

[2]Ben-Sasson, H. H. (ed.), (1985). *A History of The Jewish People.* Cambridge: Harvard University Press.

[3]*Arenda, Encyclopedia Judaica.* Retrieved June 9, 2016 from http://www.jewishvirtuallibrary.org/jsource/judaica/ejud_0002_0002_0_01275.html

Poland, Ukraine and southern Russia. At the time, almost 160,000 Jews lived in the Grand Duchy of Lithuania.[4]

The Pale's Jewish population not only grew rapidly, but changed as more mystical religious practices, such as Hasidism, migrated north from southern Russia. But Lithuanian Jewry resisted those shifts. The area, in fact, was known for its rigorous Talmudic scholars, high levels of literacy and a network of well-respected yeshivot. Those academies, according to historian Dov Levin, "profoundly influenced the shape of 19th- and 20th-century Orthodox Judaism."

Vištytis sat at the furthest western edge of The Pale, on the shores of one of the largest lakes in the region. Jews had first settled in the town in 1589. "An estate owner by the name of Jesmantas permitted them to settle in the town and allocated for them a lot for building a synagogue and another lot for a cemetery," according to a family history by JewishGen. "The Jews were subject to the rule of the estate owner."[5]

Some Jewish residents built roads, repaired mills and constructed dams, while others processed hog bristles for brushes, ran small shops or orchestrated trade with towns in nearby Prussia.

This was the community where Abraham Pearlstein, who was born in Vištytis in the middle of the 19th century, and Goldie Rudnitsky, whose family lived in a town about 35 kilometres away, settled down to start a family. The couple owned a cattle

---

[4]Levin, D. (2011, March 14). Lithuania. YIVO Encyclopedia of Jews in Eastern Europe. Retrieved June 7, 2016, from http://www.yivoencyclopedia.org/article.aspx/Lithuania.

[5]Rosin, J. (Translation by Pinkas Hakefhillot Lita). (1996). Vistytis— Encyclopedia of Jewish Communities in Lithuania (Vistytis, Lithuania). Retrieved from http://www.jewishgen.org/yizkor/pinkas_lita/lit_00260.html.

farm just beyond the town limits. According to Marlene Matlow's genealogical research, Abraham sold meat and cattle to wholesalers in both Lithuania and Germany (the border was under a kilometre away), while Goldie worked in the fields and looked after what would became a large family, with 10 sons.

About 3,000 people lived in and around Vištytis at the end of the 19th century, including about 500 Jewish families (Greater Lithuania's Jewish population by then had ballooned to almost 760,000). The town, resident Jacob Rubenstein recalls in his autobiography, "was laid out symmetrically with the market square as the hub ... The streets radiated from each of its four corners at right angles to each other." His memoir paints a picture of a rustic community where most streets were either dirt or paved with cobblestones. The frame houses were built with heavy wooden beams and steeped pitched roofs, and used moss or dirt for insulation. None had toilets or running water, but the Jews of Vištytis owned and operated a public bathhouse with a large mikvah at the bottom of a steep staircase, for ritual cleansing.

Each home had a brick stove that burned blocks of peat. Out back were chicken coops, outhouses, manure piles, various types of farm equipment and a prized vegetable garden or a plot of fruit trees. Nature, in fact, was never far away. The windows of his house, writes Rubenstein, had no screens, so the tiny rooms filled with swarms of black flies in the summer. In the winter, double panes helped to keep out the cold but trapped the air inside, rendering the dwelling stale and foul smelling.

Contributing to the smell inside were the kerosene lamps used to provide lighting, albeit sparingly, because of the high cost of the fuel. Rubenstein recalls a curious custom relating to the matter of lighting in Vištytis. "Since Jewish boys had to stay in their Hebrew schools till 8 o'clock in the evening," he writes, "they had to furnish the kerosene for the school lamps in the fall and winter when the sun set early. Each day, some boy had to bring a pint of kerosene to school. Many a time I walked to school in the wintertime, carrying my books and vesper (evening lunch) in one hand and a bottle of kerosene in the other."

MARLENE MATLOW

FAMILY HISTORY

MATERNAL GRANDFATHER

Great Grandfather, _ABRAHAM_ Pearlstein, was a German citizen, but was born in Vistinitz, Lithuania, which was sometimes Poland, sometimes Germany and sometimes Lithuania. He died of a brain tumor in 1911 and is buried in a cemetery in Vistinitz.

Great Grandmother, ~~Lena~~ _GOLDIE_ Myerson, was born in _____, which is about 35 km. from Vistinitz. She died in 1915, at the age of 56, of cancer, and is buried somewhere in Lithuania.

Great Grandfather and Grandmother Pearlstein had ten children, their names were _BARNEY_, _HARRY_, _Leif (Harold)_, _LOUIS, PHILIP, DAVE_ — — — — _HARRY -NEUFRMDLAP_, all of them boys. The farm they lived on was about 30 acres in size and the business was cattle and farming. Grandfather _ABRAHAM_ sold meat and cattle wholesale on both sides of the

My grandfather was one of 10 boys and my mission was to find all their names.

The nostalgia of Rubenstein's recollection about those lamps sits uncomfortably next to the story of the devastating fire that consumed most of the village in 1910—an anecdote that loomed large in Al's recollections of his own father's early life in the old country.

According to an account by Mendel Sudarski on JewishGen.org,[6] Kaiser Wilhelm had a large palace and retreat on the opposite side of the lake from Vištytis's shore; he would travel there by yacht for the annual hunt. "Learning that the pretty

_____

[6]Sudarski, M. A Town that Kaiser Wilhelm Helped to Rebuild. Retrieved June 14, 2016 from http://www.geocities.ws/kociubaitis/Vishtytis_sudarsky.htm.

town located on the other side of the lake opposite his yacht had burned," Sudarski recounts, "his heart filled with pity, or maybe eagerness at seeing a burned-out Jewish town. One day he arrived in Vishtinetz with his retinue. It was Yom Kippur and there was no prior warning announcing his visit."

The town was eerily quiet, not just because of the high holidays but because some residents, including many Jews, had already pulled up stakes and left their homes in the wake of the pogroms that had swept across Russia and parts of Eastern Europe beginning in 1905.

Summoning Vištytis's remaining Jews from synagogue, he informed them that he would contribute a large sum to a reconstruction fund and then urge his cousin, Czar Nicholas II, to also provide cash. Many prominent Jews, including my great-grandfather Abraham (Harry's father), signed a proclamation thanking the Kaiser for his munificence. Sudarski points out that while the unexpected gift generated much positive publicity for the Kaiser, the money in the end wasn't sufficient to properly rebuild a community that would continue shrinking in the years to come.

At the time of the fire, as it happens, several of Abraham and Goldie Pearlstein's older sons had already left Vištytis and the family farm, joining the mass Jewish exodus toward Western Europe and the United States. Al's father Harry was just nine years old—a young boy in a dying village, who would soon endure the unexpected departure of yet another family member.

CHAPTER 2: HARRY TWO

My grandparents, me and my family at my brother Geoff's bar mitzvah, Toronto, 1970.

During the summer of 1978, Alan Groedel, a friend from the Huntsville camp where I had briefly worked, invited me to visit his home in a prosperous suburb of Cleveland. I had just finished high school and relished the prospect of travelling without my parents. But a trip by train or plane wasn't in the cards, financially.

As it happened, my grandfather Harry had a cousin in Cleveland he wanted to visit. So, we set off. Me, a young-looking 19-year-old eagerly anticipating a weekend of hard partying, and Harry, who at 76 was balding, barrel-chested and gruff—the kind of man who'd nurse a soggy cigar stub for the better part of an hour.

We must have come across as an odd couple when we pulled into customs at the Peace Bridge, with me behind the wheel of Harry's brown and bruised sedan.

"Where are you headed today?" the border official asked.

"Cleveland," I replied nervously. He didn't believe me at first, and I had to explain the journey a second time before we were waved through. For the next few hours, Harry and I motored westward along Interstate 90. It was a sweltering afternoon and his gas-guzzling Chevy didn't have air conditioning. He dutifully canvassed me for details about what was going on with my brother and sisters and our cousins; I, in turn, inquired about the volunteer work he did with his synagogue. (Among his more unusual duties was performing the mitzvah of closing the eyes of someone who had just died.) But my grandfather wasn't a natural conversationalist, so the long drive was marked by long silences. The exchanges I remember as vividly as any other featured cynical barbs, crude Yiddish slang or bitter recriminations directed at his closest family members, including his son, Al.

When we eventually reached Cleveland, I took an exit marked downtown. We soon found ourselves on a broad avenue leading toward the city's football stadium, on the shore of Lake Erie. The street, I noticed, was lined with empty warehouses and boarded-up storefronts. As we ventured further into the city, Harry pointed out the dodgy-looking characters loitering on the cracked, litter-strewn sidewalks.

I quickly realized we had strayed into the wrong part of town.

"Hang on," I told Harry, and made a sharp U-turn, squealing the tires as I stepped on the gas. My grandfather lurched toward the passenger window.

As we sped back to the highway and the affluent Cleveland suburb where his cousin lived, Harry sat in shocked silence for several minutes. And Harry was not a man who shocked easily.

"What," he finally asked, "was the fancy driving for?"

I looked over at him and realized he seemed vaguely impressed. Indeed, for the rest of his life, my crusty and acerbic grandfather would always joke about my fancy driving on that trip to Cleveland whenever we'd see one another.

* * *

Growing up, I saw a lot of my maternal grandfather because he lived with us, in his own part of our home in North York. My siblings and I tended to see less of Harry and our paternal grandmother, Sarah, a quiet woman who rarely ventured out and seemed to suffer from some unspecified psychological condition. They lived in a modest and musty-smelling house on Roberta Drive, a crescent connected to a gently curving street near a shopping plaza at Bathurst and Lawrence. The house had a standalone garage with a gas lawnmower. The backyard smelled of freshly cut grass mixed with the oily aroma of their mower.

My sister Melissa recalls visiting them on Sundays, sometimes for dinner and often for a game of cards. She says Sarah would, on some visits, quietly beckon her to come into their bedroom so she could slip Melissa a $10 bill as a secret gift. (Sarah died in the summer of 1982 in a nursing home, just before her seventy-eighth birthday.)

In June, 1980, I took my girlfriend Sharon, who later became my wife, to the house to introduce her to Harry. It was late in the afternoon and although the sitting room faced west, it was relatively dark because of the awnings over the windows. Harry greeted us and we went to sit down. The house was hot and stuffy.

We made small talk and Harry offered us a drink. As he went into the kitchen, I decided to turn on a pair of lamps on either side of my grandparents' threadbare couch. But when I flicked the switch on the wall, nothing happened.

"You need new bulbs," I called to Harry.

He came out of the kitchen, opened a drawer in a chest and pulled out a single 60W bulb, which he twisted into the socket of one of the lamps. The implication was clear: one was sufficient. Sharon and I finished that initial get-to-know-you visit in the twilight of his legendary thriftiness.

As Melissa says, "Warm and cuddly, he wasn't."

But my brother Geoff offers up another set of memories about our grandfather, pointing out that he was famous for his oddball expressions. A "sailor's farewell" meant f--k off, while "rickets" was his all-purpose word for disease. "If anyone had an illness of almost any type, from feeling under the weather, a broken arm or leg, or was even seriously ill," Geoff recounts, "Harry would simply say that 'so and so had the rickets.'" That piece of verbal shorthand was adopted whole cloth by his grandchildren. We all use that word with Harry's meaning.

Prices also triggered Harry's unique turns of phrase. He would always ask us what this or that cost. Regardless of what the item was, he'd be aghast at the amount. "I'd shoot myself rather than pay that type of money."

Then, for several years after Harry sold his house and moved into a B'nai Brith senior's home on Bathurst Street near Earl Bales Park, Geoff dropped by for what turned out to be a run of Saturday afternoon visits that took place throughout the final eight years of Harry's life. When Geoff arrived—and later with his wife Linda and their young sons—Harry would pull out a bottle of Canadian Club and they'd share a couple of shots of whiskey while playing a quick round of gin rummy.

Harry, Geoff recalls, greeted him with a hail of nicknames. "Doctor," "General," "Professor," plus various Yiddishisms including a strange but ritually repeated wisecrack, "How's your macher?" (the word is slang for a male body part). Later, when Geoff and Linda brought along their young sons, the two boys, scarcely out of pull-ups, would charge at Harry as they burst into the flat. "Hey Zaide," they'd laugh, "how's your macher?"

"He'd light up like a Christmas tree," Geoff recalls. "Those were pretty precious moments. He was lonely, and happy to see us."

* * *

Today, when I go over my memories of Harry, I can't say that his tough demeanor comes as much of a surprise. He had a difficult life that spanned two continents and included abandonment, war, immigration, poverty, family illness, relocation and perhaps, deep down but never expressed, disappointment.

"My mother called him a gypsy," recalls my Aunt Gloria, Harry's only daughter. "He was restless." He retired young and spent the second half of his life hunkered down in a state of self-imposed austerity, as if always bracing for the next hardship.

Back in 1912, scarcely a year after the death of my great-grandfather Abraham Pearlstein, his wife Goldie packed her bags and left Vištytis. She headed to Boston, a distant city in golden America where several of her 10 sons lived. Goldie was 52. Harry, the youngest, remained in Vištytis—a 10-year-old in a village that was dying as its residents decamped to safer harbours.

Goldie lived in Boston for two years, with one of her sons, and then returned to Vištytis in 1914, bringing with her a trunk filled with gifts for Harry's bar mitzvah.

The family lore that has come down to my generation doesn't include any details about those two years in Harry's life; he certainly never spoke of it. But I find myself imagining what it must have been like for this little boy: father dead, mother and most of his brothers far away, an uncertain and provisional future. Goldie's return, moreover, turned out to be tragically brief. She succumbed to cancer in 1915, by which point World War I was in full swing, and Lithuania's constantly shifting borders seemed again to be in play.

During the war, Harry left Vištytis and went to live in a town about 20 kilometres away. He spent some time in a German work camp. After the Armistice, he made his way back to his hometown, to live with a cousin. But territorial hostilities between Poland and Lithuania resumed soon after, in 1919, as part of the destabilization of the national boundaries along the Soviet Union's western frontier.

Harry briefly served with the Lithuanian army, whose recruiters had fanned out across the countryside, rounding up conscripts. The fighting didn't last long, but the oppressive instability didn't end with the cessation of hostilities. As Poland, Germany and the Soviet Union jostled for land and political control in the 1920s, the local economy floundered. My father, Al, grew up with Harry's stories about runaway inflation that rendered earnings and savings worthless and prompted bank runs. Harry brought his suspicion of banks—but little else—with him when he finally crossed the Atlantic.

In 1925, at the age of 23, Harry Pearlstein had had enough. He made his way to Hamburg, Germany and bought a ticket for a seat on a ship bound for America, intending to join his brothers in Boston. But when the boat stopped to refuel in Sydney, Nova Scotia, fate intervened in Harry's life, as it has done with so many immigrants who fled political turmoil in hopes of a better life.

The ship had come across from Europe the year before loaded with illegal or undocumented refugees. This time, Al recounts, Canadian immigration officials told the captain to deposit his human cargo in Newfoundland or take them back to Hamburg. The captain steamed to the Rock. As my Aunt Gloria Houser, Harry's only daughter, recalls, "He was given a choice of stopping in St. John's or going back to Europe. He had nothing."

* * *

During his tumultuous exodus, Harry Pearlstein had fled the political and economic instability of eastern Europe but found himself alone in a remote but storied port of call struggling with its own grinding commercial crisis.

At the time, Newfoundland functioned as a self-governing colony of the United Kingdom. The island's 270,000 residents[7] generated most of their income from the bountiful North Atlantic fishery, while investors from Europe and America flocked to the province to tap the region's rich mineral resources.

Yet despite those abundant natural resources, the colony had stumbled through the years following World War I with a "dangerously fragile" economy.[8] During the war, the House of Assembly insisted on raising a Newfoundland regiment to send to the battlefields of France.

But the cost of loyalty proved to be steep and left a debt overhang on the government's books long after the fighting stopped. Making matters worse, Newfoundland's private railway

---

[7]Section A. Population and Vital Statistics Retrieved from http://www.stats.gov.nl.ca/Publications/Historical/PDF/SectionA.pdf.

[8]Higgins, J. (2007). Newfoundland and Labrador Heritage website. Events leading up to the Great Depression. Retrieved from http://www.heritage.nf.ca/articles/politics/depression-origin.php.

company was hit with crippling financial problems, forcing the colonial government to nationalize its assets and operations. Then, in the early 1930s, world fish prices plunged, sending Newfoundland's export revenues into a free fall. "By 1933, the country owed close to $100 million and faced bankruptcy," according to a provincial history.[9] The following year, the British government installed a caretaker government.

Besides all the economic gloom, Harry had ended up in a place with a tiny Jewish community. While Joseph De la Penha, a Dutch Jewish merchant adventurer, had claimed Labrador for England in 1677, the first recorded Jewish residents only traced back to the early 1900s. By the time Harry Pearlstein stepped onto the wharves near Water Street, Newfoundland was home to scarcely more than 200 Jews, most of them living in St. John's.[10] The close-knit community, mostly merchants, couldn't attract a rabbi or afford a parochial school.

Harry soon found a job in St. John's, working as a butcher. It was a natural choice, as he'd grown up on his father's cattle farm. Not long after he started, a young woman named Sarah Sheffman came in to buy some meat. The Sheffman family had been in St. John's since the turn of the century, after Sarah's father Morris emigrated from a shtetl in the Pale of Settlement (now Belarus). They soon married, and Al, their first child, was born in 1927.

Two years later, with Sarah expecting their second child, Harry moved the family up to Bonavista, a remote outport town at the far end of a winding, 300-kilometre road. (Al's brother, David,

---

[9]Higgins, J. (2007). Newfoundland and Labrador Heritage website. Great Depression - Impacts on the Working Class. Retrieved from http://www.heritage.nf.ca/articles/politics/depression-impacts.php.

[10]Medjuck, S. (1986). *Jews of Atlantic Canada* (St. John's).

was born in 1929 and his sister, Gloria, in 1931.) For the next four years, Harry ran a succession of small businesses, including a slaughterhouse, on their property. The barn, Al recalls, was built around a large grain hopper. Once, he and a friend made a game of throwing lit matches into the hopper and soon the barn had caught fire. "My mother hid me from my father for a couple of days," Al remembers. "She realized he'd be pretty pissed off."

Edward Sheffman, Al's cousin, recalls that Harry was one of the very few people with a car, a 1931 Chrysler which he pressed into service as a delivery vehicle. "He took out the back seat and carried cows to the butcher where they'd be slaughtered." The car, Al adds, had no brakes. "There were no mechanics around. After six months, there were only two ways to stop the car: with a flat tire, or—and don't laugh—to go into a fence."

Harry also met someone who would become a pivotal figure in the history of the colony. A few years after he returned to the Rock from a stint in journalism in New York City, Joey Smallwood decided to stand for election in the provincial riding of Bonavista South. The future Father of Confederation would come into Harry's store, and the two men would kibitz, playing cards and drinking together. "I think we were the only Jews in Bonavista," Al says. "Joey remembered my father."

Yet the collapsing cod prices and the wider fallout from the Great Depression doomed Harry's business ventures. "In 1931 and 1932," recalls Al, "everyone went broke in the retail business and no one could get credit."

In 1934, Harry cut his losses and moved the family back to St. John's. He borrowed $1,200 from one of his wife's brothers and opened up a dry goods store at 308 Water St., near the wharves—a business he grandly named "Broadway Bargains Store."

This store was once the location of Broadway Bargains. My dad and his family lived on the upper floors.

Later in life, Harry would tell Al a fable about the nature of calculated business risk—a story about two brothers surviving the hyperinflation of Germany in the 1920s. One always put his savings in the bank, while the other, who liked a drink, spent his savings on liquor, stashing the empties in the attic. Yet when the value of the German mark collapsed, the drinking brother had something—bottles—to sell, while the savings brother had nothing because his deposits had lost their value, Harry explained. "Maybe he was letting me know that you can't be too smart by being too cautious all the time," Al says. "He had to take risks."

Harry's store was about 30' x 40' with mostly women's clothing, but also some menswear—all of it purchased on twice-a-year buying trips to clothing manufacturers in Montreal. For all of his experience cutting meat, Harry adapted well to the shmata trade, often standing on the sidewalk in front of the shop, corralling in the sailors and fishermen who would wander along a street lined by shops, several of them run by the city's other Jewish merchants.

In St. John's during the Depression, Harry must have been a bit of a character: with his light hair, broad chest and powerful arms, he spoke a broken, Yiddish-inflected English, but that didn't stop him from chatting up his customers. He always had a bottle of something strong in the drawer behind the till and would be happy to share a shot or two with a man who had been out in the North Atlantic for days or weeks at a time. "He had a knack for talking to people," says Edward Sheffman, Al's cousin. None of them, moreover, cared that he was Jewish: anti-Semitism simply wasn't an issue in Newfoundland.

The family, meanwhile, lived on two floors above the store in a spare apartment without central heating. Gloria, Al's sister, remembers that they relied on the stove in the kitchen for warmth. There was a dining room and three bedrooms on the third floor, but little in the way of décor or ornamentation, apart from some family photos on the walls. "My father," she says, "was not a spender, he was a saver."

Al, Gloria and their brother David attended St. John's local Protestant parochial schools—Bishop Spencer College and Bishop Feild College. Edward recalls visiting the apartment with his family on Sunday afternoons to play cards and listen to Harry tell funny stories or make jokes.

"He was a wonderful guy. He could always do something to make you laugh."

By the late 1930s, in fact, Broadway Bargains had become a thriving and profitable enterprise. The looming prospect of war in Europe proved to be a boon to strategically important port cities like St. John's. After more than a decade of penury and failed businesses, Harry and Sarah's financial fortunes finally seemed to have stabilized and they could begin to save for their children's future.

But that prosperity would be blunted by a parent's worst nightmare: an alarming illness in their eldest child, Al.

CHAPTER 3: AL AND THE ASTHMA YEARS

From the time my three siblings and I were little until the present day, we have always loved sports and fitness and understood the importance of physical well-being for a balanced lifestyle.

Between the ages of 7 and 13, I played hockey competitively. Geoff's sport was football; Melissa's was tennis. As an adult, Debbie became very serious about cardio workouts, such as spinning. When we were all young, we skied and swam and played golf—often, in the case of the latter activities, at the Donalda Club, which my parents joined after they moved to Don Mills in the mid-1950s. My siblings and I have all kept up these habits of the body, investing the necessary time to stay fit and healthy. And we have sought to impart these values to our own children.

I don't have to look too far or too deeply to understand the source of our shared devotion to these pastimes. As long as I can remember, Al has been part of this picture, enjoying squash and golf, driving me to hockey games at the local rink, or hitting a tennis ball around with Melissa on the street in front of our house.

My sister Debbie offers up another memory. "He'd always exercise in the morning," she says, noting his lifelong habit of doing dozens of pushups in his pyjamas after he woke up. I remember he used to show us how he could do marine pushups, which include a clap on the way up. "My father can still wear his naval uniform from when he was 21," she marvels. "How many guys can do that?"

In his teens, Al recounts, he'd heard about the famed bodybuilder Charles Atlas and was inspired to follow his advice of a daily regimen of calisthenics. "I've been doing pushups for 75 years. I don't think I've missed too many days."

"He always looked after himself," adds Wayne Samsoondar, a North York physician who performed a risky operation on Al in 2003 to surgically remove a prostate tumor rather than treating it with radiation. "The only reason I operated on him is because he was fitter than most 60-year-olds, although he was 76," Samsoondar observes. "Mentally, physically, he was in great shape."

* * *

Al came to his lifelong commitment to fitness the hard way, through illness. Those who have experienced debilitating or incapacitating infirmity, and have then recovered, understand that good health is a gift to be treasured and protected, and never taken for granted.

For Al, as a youngster growing up in damp and draughty Depression-era Newfoundland, contending with poor health was a fact of life. Soon after Harry relocated his family back to St. John's, Al, then about five, developed the symptoms of severe and unrelenting asthma—a condition that not only shackled his childhood but, in many ways, changed the course of his life.

Gloria Houser, Al's sister, and Edward Sheffman, his cousin, remember the extreme coughing and the way those bouts drained Al of strength when he should have been running around with his friends.

"He couldn't walk up the stairs [leading to the apartment over Broadway Bargains]," Gloria says. "He would sit over the table and cough all night long."

"He almost died several times," Edward adds. "He was very thin. He was sickly. He didn't grow strong. I don't think he had much of a childhood."

At Bishop Feild College, the private Church of England-affiliated school in St. John's, Al couldn't participate in sports or other physical activities so he spent much of his spare time reading or studying. "It didn't bother me," he insists, noting that he developed powerful abdominal muscles from the coughing. "I never felt sorry for myself. I was able to concentrate on my schoolwork." But, as Al confided to a family friend many years later, he sometimes feared that he wouldn't survive to see his teens.

His parents grew increasingly anxious about the chronic condition that seemed to be impairing the development of their eldest son. "My father tried to do whatever he could to help me," Al says. "Of course, it was hard on him."

As happens with an intractable childhood disease, Al's parents desperately sought alternative treatments—burning herbs in an attempt to open up the boy's bronchial passages, and taking him to a local physician for adrenalin shots. But when the doctor warned that these injections could lead to a heart condition, Harry decided to look further afield for medical advice. He contacted one of his brothers in Boston and, in 1939, ventured down to the

Massachusetts city so Al could see a specialist. But even the U.S. physician's treatment didn't reverse the asthma.

The trip wasn't all business. "One day," Al says, "my cousin Gloria, who was nine or 10 years older than me, took me downtown and we went shopping in Filene's Basement, a discount department store. That was quite an adventure for me after coming from a small town like St. John's. I remember having a fancy ice-cream cone. She showed me what was going on and I'll never forget it."

Not long after they returned, Harry realized he'd have to take drastic action, removing Al from the damp Maritime air that greatly exacerbated his wheezing. He contacted Tanchem (a.k.a. Harry), his older brother in Los Angeles, and arranged for Al to stay with one of Tanchem's four daughters, to convalesce. Al was 13.

On May 8, 1940, Harry and Al boarded a train that took them from St. John's all the way along the south shore of Newfoundland to Channel-Port aux Basques, where they transferred to the ferry that crosses to Sydney, Nova Scotia. Over the next four days, they traveled across the continent, sharing a berth in a train that traveled to Boston, Chicago and on to Los Angeles. Al remembers little of the journey, except that they stopped for a day in the Windy City to visit a relative.

The two Pearlsteins arrived in Los Angeles five days later. Al immediately noticed the weather—clear blue skies, fresh air (even though the city even then had smog) and warm, dry days. Harry left Al with his cousin Edith, the third of Tanchem's four daughters. Just 29, she lived with her husband Sidney Cohen at 2525 Boulder Avenue, in the ground floor apartment of a bungalow in a comfortable middle-class area in east Los Angeles that was home to a large population of Jewish families.

Edith and Sidney didn't have children; she worked in a supermarket as a product demonstrator, and her husband was in the meat business. They soon introduced the fragile little boy to Edith's sisters and brothers-in-law and all their children, Al's new extended family. To those robust American kids, he must have seemed like something of an apparition—just 65 pounds and only 4'7". "My cousin said I looked like Casper the Friendly Ghost because I was so pale," Al recounts.

Marlene and Al on Ocean Beach, in Santa Monica, fall, 1940.

Soon after he arrived, Edith's older sister took Al to an asthma specialist who had a clinic on Sunset Boulevard. "He looked at me and said, 'You have to go to the TB camp in the mountains outside Los Angeles,'" Al says.

As in many North American cities, Los Angeles in the early years of the 20th century had mounted an aggressive fight against tuberculosis, an infectious disease associated with poverty, slum conditions and immigration.

Treatment facilities had popped up in several locations around the region. The Olive View Sanatorium, situated in a Los Angeles suburb nestled in the rugged but scrubby foothills surrounding the city, was a sprawling, 300-acre facility that housed over a thousand patients by the 1940s. According to a 1995 account in the *Los*

Angeles Times,[11] many patients couldn't see their family members and were subjected to aggressive, experimental treatments as well as the accepted regimen of outdoor rest.

Al, for his part, was sent to a smaller sanatorium in Tujunga, another mountain suburb later annexed by L.A. Because of its altitude and fresh air, Los Angeles respirologists sent asthmatics to the area as well. After a few months, Al was already making progress and seemed well enough to return to Edith and Sidney's home. That September, he was able to enroll in the local high school named, appropriately enough, after Theodore Roosevelt, who himself had overcome severe childhood asthma to become a famously energetic soldier, naturalist and politician.

When Al showed the school's administrators his transcript from Bishop Feild, they were "surprised," as Al recalls, to see that he'd already studied algebra, chemistry, French, Latin and physics, even though he was just 13. ("We had English schoolmasters and they came over because they couldn't get jobs in England, so the school in those days was good.") He did especially well in arithmetic, and had also skipped a grade in Newfoundland. While Al attributes his academic prowess to the fact that he spent more time studying because he couldn't participate in sports, an IQ test administered by Theodore Roosevelt H. S. showed he had scored an impressive 141, sufficient to warrant placement in Grade 11.

"I had good marks but I was socially very immature and very small," he recalls. The school eventually recommended that he repeat Grade 11 and take a variety of non-academic classes, like drafting, typing and music.

At the time, Theodore Roosevelt H. S. was a huge place, with

---

[11]Leovy, J. (Oct. 28, 1995). *Los Angeles Times*. Breathing New Life: Olive View. Retrieved from http://articles.latimes.com/1995-10-28/local/me-62120_1_olive-view.

about 4,000 students from a wide range of backgrounds—Jewish, Japanese, Hispanic and African-American. Al recalls that the teens from Japanese-American families disappeared after the December, 1941 attack on Pearl Harbour, as the U.S. government sent thousands to internment camps on the orders of President Franklin D. Roosevelt.

Al, far right, with Roosevelt High's math club, 1942.

In those first two years, Al spent his free time playing basketball and touch football on the street with local boys. He joined the high school's math club and, according to the comments in his yearbook, helped many of his classmates with their homework. "Albert," as he was called, quickly became known as the smart kid in his grade. "To my irresistible little weasel," one wrote, jokingly, "may you grow old and become an average student." But many of the students who signed Al's yearbook noted his stature—not in an unfriendly way, but enough to suggest that this feature would determine how he'd be remembered. As one wrote, typically, "Best of luck to a swell little classmate."

"He never had anything negative to say about being a small, slight guy in those teenage years," Melissa observes. Those remarks, Al confirms, "didn't bother me." The reason: "Within a year, I felt better." He'd begun to gain weight, grow and fill out, largely because his debilitating coughing and bouts of breathlessness had all but disappeared. With his new lease on life, the increasingly obsolete labels had little power to inflict pain.

Al's keepsakes from his years in the Canadian Naval Reserve.

* * *

My dad has a collection of ephemera he's saved from the summers he spent, between 1946 and 1948, in Canada's Naval Reserve. The items include a tiny cloth-covered shore pass book, an epaulet, discharge papers and a postcard showing a map of North America marked with the 12,000-mile route that the H.M.S. Sheffield, his ship, took as it sailed from Bermuda to Vancouver and back again between June and August, 1948.

What's most captivating about these keepsakes are the photos—wallet-sized black-and-white snapshots of robust young men who look like they are thoroughly enjoying themselves as they pose on the decks of various destroyers, with the exotic mountains and palm trees of Mexico and Central America in the distance.

Al on deck of the HMS Sheffield, 1948.

Most of the pictures include Al: tanned and buff, the very picture of good health. In one, he leans rakishly against the guide-wires on a ship's deck, in only white shorts and sandals, revealing his trim and muscular torso. In another, taken in 1947, he stands between two other sailors. Al is wearing his sailor's shore-leave outfit—a navy blue top with white trim and flared slacks. On the back of the picture, written in his small, precise hand, he's noted his comrades' names: Stan and Nixon. Behind them are the ship's cannons and its control tower.

Al served in Mess 24, with a group of about 14 professional British seamen who decided to re-name him Canada. They worked and ate together, and took their shore leaves as a group. The days mainly featured heavy ship work—Al says he missed most of the Panama Canal on one journey because his mess had to haul dozens of sacks of rotting beans out of a storage area four levels below the main deck. But there were also interludes, for example when visiting dignitaries would inspect the troops or host receptions. The experience, he recalls, "was a wonderful way to learn about the real world after having a relatively sheltered upbringing."

Typically, Al undersells what had changed in his world. In just six years, he'd traveled a vast distance, from the sickly, underweight child deposited in 1940 with a Los Angeles relative into the strong, independent young man who grins across the years from those photographs. If nothing else, the images offer a vindication of Harry Pearlstein's courageous but difficult decision to send his eldest son away from an environment that seemed to be crushing the boy before he ever got started in life.

After Al graduated from Theodore Roosevelt H.S. in Los Angeles in 1943, he enrolled at the University of California, Los Angeles (UCLA), with a general idea of going into medicine. As he says, he wanted to learn more about asthma and someday help others suffering from the same condition. Al enrolled in pre-med courses.

He initially drove to the university every morning with a friend, but the journey between East Los Angeles, where Edith and Sidney lived, to UCLA's campus in Westwood, consumed four hours each day. It was the tediousness of that experience which taught Al the importance of working efficiently and not wasting time—organizational habits of mind that he retained throughout his life and career.

In 1945, shortly before the end of the Second World War, Al received dramatic news from his family in Newfoundland. Harry had decided to move to Canada (Newfoundland was still a British colony). After considering Montreal and Vancouver, he chose Toronto because Sarah had a friend who vouched for the city.

While Broadway Bargains was thriving and the Pearlsteins could finally live comfortably and build up their savings, Harry felt he had to move for religious reasons: as Al, David and Gloria reached young adulthood, he wanted them to find Jewish spouses and reckoned that the community in St. John's was just too small.

For Al, his family's move to Toronto raised the prospect of a return to Canada for him, as well. "When I knew that, I thought I'd try to get into the University of Toronto. I missed my family. I had never thought of staying in L.A. forever."

But much had changed since he had left Newfoundland five years earlier. During all that time, he'd not seen his mother Sarah, or his two siblings, David and Gloria, who were 16 and 14 years old, respectively. "We missed him," says Gloria. "I didn't get to see him because it was a big, big trip. There were no planes. We really looked forward to his return."

Harry, for his part, had traveled to L.A. twice a year by train—trips that lasted for a few weeks. The details and sentiments around Harry's visits have slipped away—Al: "I never really understood or asked him many questions, and he wasn't forthcoming"—but the distance had forced the teen to become more self-sufficient. "[The reunions] didn't affect me much because I was busy at school," he shrugs. "I was basically too young to analyze it or think it through."

"His storytelling was void of whether this was an emotionally wrenching thing," Melissa says. "He had no choice." Still, she has found herself wondering on occasion what it was like for her father to be so far from home and his parents during those formative years. "Who would he talk to when he had a problem?" The experience, Gloria confirms, made Al grow up faster. "He couldn't lean on his parents, especially his strong father."

Al agreed that the experience of being separated from his family was one that strengthened him not just physically, but emotionally, perhaps in the way that Harry had had to fend for himself as a young man in Lithuania. "I go back to my father," he says. "He started from scratch. His parents died when he was young." By that point in his own life, Al adds, "I was used to doing things on my own."

When he did settle back in with his family in Toronto—the Pearlsteins lived in several homes for the first few years in the city, finally purchasing a house in a new subdivision near Lawrence and Bathurst—there was initially a sense of great relief, Gloria recalls. "It was a happy time. That was our goal, being together again." One of the first things Al did upon coming home was to buy his little sister a bicycle.

Yet Al discovered problems he had not been fully aware of when he'd left five years earlier. Despite years of commercial success with his Water Street dry goods store, Harry had discovered that the clothing business in Toronto was much more competitive. He reverted to a familiar commodity—meat. Harry opened a succession of butcher shops—on Dundas East around Parliament Street, and then on Bloor West near Ossington Avenue, with a store called City Meat Market—but he struggled to establish himself and to turn a profit, despite the fact that he often worked 70 or 80 hours a week. (He eventually opted to retire very young, at the age of 52.)

Meanwhile, Al's mother, Sarah, was suffering from a somewhat debilitating depression, and his younger brother David, who worked in Harry's butcher shops, also seemed to be afflicted with the condition. "He had to get treatment and my father's English wasn't good, so I had to go to the doctor's with him to explain and help get those problems solved," Al says. But he felt somewhat detached from his family after five years away. "I was sort of an outsider, and I never had time or really thought about the social interaction." Gloria, however, remembers him as a "guiding force in our family. Strong, right from the beginning."

Upon his return, Al enrolled at the University of Toronto (U of T), although he couldn't get into medical school because those slots were reserved, in the immediate aftermath of the war, for returning veterans. Initially, he opted to take science courses, such as physiology and biochemistry, but, as Al commented early on, "I knew that even with extra effort, there was probably no chance that I could do well in the course ... so I decided to switch gears."

Just a few weeks into his first term, Al switched up his whole course load, taking history, German and other arts courses. By the second year, he also enrolled in commerce and finance program. "The courses we had on accounting, economic history and economic theory were all intriguing."

Throughout his life, Al has promoted to my siblings and me, and indeed to most young people he meets, the importance of a broad education that includes the arts, history and politics. In his own case, he was particularly interested in the courses on the history of markets, and also the broader dynamics that drive civilizations.

One of his courses was given by Harold Innis, the influential professor of political economy responsible for the so-called "staples theory," which described how the fluctuations in global demand for core commodities had a profound impact on Canada's economy. Al also heard Innis deliver his "empire and communications" lectures, in which he argued how different modes of communication play an important role in determining the fates of nations and empires.

Yet Al, as he is the first to admit, didn't exactly have his nose pressed to the academic grindstone as he'd had when he was younger and unwell. At U of T, he belonged to a loose-knit group of friends, none of whom belonged to fraternities. They liked to play pool at a hall on Eglinton Avenue and dubbed themselves the XTC Club (the name came from a 1933 film, "Ecstasy," featuring the movie star Hedy Lamarr). They gave Al a quirky but enduring nickname, Duke, for the odd way he pronounced the word duck when exhorting his buddies to "duck up to the pool hall" for a game. Al also spent a lot of time playing bridge, even when he was supposed to be in class—up to five hours a day.

One of the students he met and befriended at U of T went on to achieve a major breakthrough in Canadian politics. Leonard Braithwaite, the son of a Barbadian father and a Jamaican mother, was born in the Kensington Market neighbourhood of Toronto in 1923, served as an engine mechanic with the Royal Canadian Air Force during the Second World War, and then enrolled in the commerce program at U of T.[12]

"He had only gone to Grade 11 in high school and when he got back from the war, because of the allowances for veterans, he barely had enough money to finish," Al recalls. "Then he came into our class for commerce and finance in September, 1946, and he became friendly with some of the Jewish fellows. We would study together." After Braithwaite graduated, he went on to

---

[12]Yarhi E. (Rev.) Leonard Braithwaite (Nov. 27, 2013). Retrieved from http://www.thecanadianencyclopedia.ca/en/article/leonard-braithwaite/.

complete an MBA at Harvard and then a law degree from Osgoode Hall. By 1960, he'd entered politics as a school trustee, and later went on to become the first black member of the Ontario legislature.

Another young man Al encountered as a student was Burke Brown, whose family owned a profitable car dealership in the west end of Toronto. "He was in psychology and was part of a group that formed an investment club called Cardinal Investments," Al says. "He was involved in trying to get people to invest in businesses."

As Al moved through his commerce and finance degree, he began to think more seriously about a career in some kind of financial field. He briefly toyed with the idea of becoming an actuary, and even made some inquiries about the profession with a contact, a consulting actuary who had articled at Great-West Life.

But he also found himself thinking about investing. And not just thinking. While still at U of T, and perhaps inspired by Burke Brown's investment club, he noticed an ad promoting a penny mining stock, in a Toronto newspaper. "I told my father that this was going to make a lot of money for him, so he bought a thousand shares at 92 cents per share." A few years later, however, the company had to re-organize and soon went out of business altogether.

It would be years before Harry finally stopped pointedly reminding Al about that botched investment, his very first buy recommendation.

CHAPTER 4: COLD CALLS

As is true for many who work in the financial services industry, I spend my days steeped in massive quantities of detailed information to ensure that I am keeping up with industry and market happenings, paying special attention to the investments I recommend to my clients. I have two large-screen computer terminals on my desk, as well as my various digital devices—smartphone, tablet, laptop. They are all equipped with sophisticated analytical software and instant access to seemingly endless databases. My firm employs highly skilled financial analysts to evaluate investment opportunities for advisors to consider for their clients. With a few keystrokes, I can diagnose what's going on with a client's portfolio and make complex calculations about rebalancing options, or provide an historical analysis about their specific portfolio performance. When it comes to data, we are blessed with an embarrassment of riches.

None of this, of course, existed on a snowy Tuesday morning in early January in 1953, when Al—then 26 and as green as could be—got into his 1949 Mercury and headed off to make the first cold call of his new career as a stockbroker.

He had spent two and a half years working as a back-office clerk at Milner Ross[13], entering the previous day's trading into the company's ledgers. It was the first job Al had found after graduating from U of T in 1950. While other entry-level clerks

---

[13]Milner Ross was a predecessor of Pitfield, Mackay, Ross & Company Limited, which later became Dominion Securities Inc. and ultimately RBC Dominion Securities Inc.

may have found the accounting work dull, Al raced through his duties and then set out to soak up as much as he could learn about how the firm worked, what its salesmen did, and the sorts of investments their clients were buying. "I started from scratch," he muses. "It was amazing what I learned there."

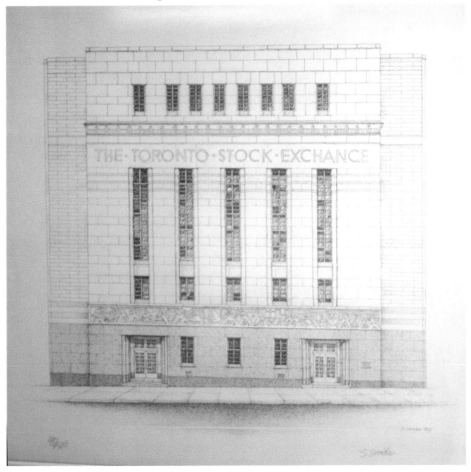

This print of original Toronto Stock Exchange on Bay St. hangs in my office.

Al's first sales foray occurred four years before Standard & Poor's introduced its index of 500 leading stocks, and 24 years before the Toronto Stock Exchange launched the TSE 300.

Early in Al's career, brokerage houses didn't employ analysts and researchers who provided buy/sell recommendations; his firm had one statistician to crunch the numbers. Indeed, besides the voluminous ledgers recording client purchases and the Dow Jones Industrial Average, someone like Al would have had to rely mainly on newspapers and business magazines for information about what was going on in the world of finance. And even those sources offered only the sparsest details.

If Al had scanned the business pages of *The Globe and Mail* the evening before his first sales mission, he would have found a long story about the latest expansion by the storied broker James Richardson & Sons, little items about life insurance policies and the pace of cheque cashing activity, several short stories about incremental developments in lead, zinc and oil production, and two tables of bond prices and maturation dates. An article with a Lethbridge dateline offered up something an enterprising stockbroker would have been able to leverage—about how Alberta oil discoveries were starting to hurt the province's coal sector. The section's last page included a graph showing monthly changes in the gold index over five years. For someone working on a trading floor today, that chart would be the only vaguely recognizable financial information in the *Globe* that morning.

To compensate, Al began to read broadly and was developing great skill in synthesizing, analyzing and discerning the subtle patterns that linked global events, economic cycles and market behaviour. During the two-and-a-half years he'd spent in the back office, for example, he had watched the TSE boom due to speculation in precious metals and energy stocks driven by the Korean War. Companies on U.S. and Canadian exchanges saw their stocks bid up 10-fold over short periods, and brokers or promoters were hustling to sell shares to investors eager to make a killing. Too often, those shares were all but worthless. "These people who were buying stocks were called the 'pooch' and the person who was selling the stock was the 'mooch'," Al recalls hearing about an alleged scam referred to as "pitching paper to the pooches."

One of those investors, as it happened, was Al's father Harry, who owned a few thousand shares of a penny mining company promoted by two brothers he'd met in 1948. "They told him that it was going to make a lot of money and it was going to go up in value." Instead, the stock crashed and then limped along for a few years until a 1951 mining boom, when the firm acquired some properties in Newfoundland. Suddenly, the trading figures began to rocket upwards. Al could see what was happening, and urged his father to sell before the law of gravity kicked in again.

He observed something else while working in that back office in 1951 and 1952. "There were no lotteries in those days, so people were speculating on mining shares and in many cases doing it on borrowed money." As a clerk, one of his duties was to adjust the interest rates the firm was charging its margin clients. As he did this painstaking work, he could see first-hand what people were buying and selling, and whether they were making a return on their investment.

"It became apparent to me quite quickly that everyone (clients and advisors) was trying to time the market and get rich fast."

What's more, by the fall of 1952, the Korean War speculative bubble had burst completely, where even blue-chip stocks like Imperial Oil and Canadian Pacific experienced a deep plunge. Al had begun the process of getting himself promoted to a sales position, but he privately resolved that he would take a more pragmatic approach to investing. Instead of looking after his investments first, his focus would always be towards his clients and ensuring that recommendations were made with the view of experiencing potential longer-term consistent growth versus investments that were considered to have higher risk/higher potential return. "I had gone through this boom and bust, so I had been through one market cycle before I started knocking on doors."

* * *

In Toronto in the early 1950s, new stockbrokers often had a difficult time breaking into the business. At the time, Ontario Securities Commission rules stated that stockbrokers had to first call on prospective clients at their workplaces; they could arrange subsequent visits at the person's home, in the evenings. (The informal professional designation has changed frequently in the intervening decades, with stockbrokers later known as brokers, salesmen, registered representatives, advisors and finally investment advisors.) Veteran stockbrokers at established firms had longstanding relationships with those in the city in a position to invest in the stock market; it was a saturated market. Some newbies, Al recalls, looked for new clients outside the city, in smaller communities like Windsor, Muskoka or Guelph. "I didn't want to go to the country," Al says. Instead, he decided to look for business in the city's rapidly growing post-war suburbs— greenfield communities such as Mimico and Scarborough, which were drawing young families as well as a new generation of entrepreneurs looking to capitalize on the post-war expansion and the baby boom. For that first sales call, in fact, he chose an industrial park in Leaside.

Al quickly learned how to identify potential clients. He'd scour and cross-reference city directories, identifying a company's key managers and executives, focusing in particular on those who owned their own home. "My premise was that if the person owned a home, at least they would be a prospect for investing." Every weekend, he would make a list of companies he planned to visit. He often tried to arrive early so he could buttonhole the potential client before their day got busy.

He had an elevator pitch he can still recite by rote. After introducing himself and the firm, Al would say, "My job is to help people with their savings. So I'm here to help you if you have any questions about how to handle your savings and plan for the future." As he recalls, "Maybe [with] one in five or one in 10, I would get a chance to talk to the person for 10 or 20 minutes, and then hopefully after that I would give them my card. And if I had an article or some follow-up material I would mail it to them and follow up in two or three months."

From observing other stockbrokers at the firm, Al knew that personal presentation was critical. While he had long since shed the visible signs of his childhood illness, Al was a young-looking 26-year-old, so he took care to dress in a dark suit to make himself look older. He also pushed back against his natural introversion, forcing himself to come across as outgoing and direct. "What you had to do, and I wasn't that good at it, was establish eye contact in the first 20 to 25 seconds and make a good impression." At one point, he took a public-speaking course so he would feel more confident and comfortable in making investment presentations to larger audiences. The best salesmen, Al had noticed, tended not to have much formal education but could bring a theatrical flair to their dealings with clients.

Finally, Al quickly realized that if he wanted to be successful, he had to be persistent. He learned not to take no for an answer, often calling on prospective clients—including those with established relationships with other brokers—multiple times. He recalls the example of one Leaside client, a senior executive with the Canadian branch of a large U.S. corporation. Al paid numerous visits to the man's office. "But I could never get in to see him."

Finally, he agreed to a meeting and apologized for all the delays. The two men discovered they got along well. He not only agreed to give Al his business, but he introduced him to other friends and co-workers. "You've got to make the calls," Al now says. "All they could do was say 'no.'"

During one such visit in the summer of 1952, a former U of T classmate named Bill Zener turned to Al after they'd finished with business and said he knew a nice young woman. "Why don't you give her a call?"

Her name was Elizabeth, or Beth, Kushner, a 23-year-old nurse from a town called Montrock, a tiny outpost north of Timmins. Her parents, Boris and Rachel, had come to Canada from Russia after the First World War, and Boris worked as a paper maker in the Abitibi mill.

After high school, Beth had worked briefly in a local dry goods store, but moved to Toronto by the time she turned 20 to pursue her dream of becoming a nurse. Beth's career decision may have been influenced by her mother's chronic poor health—a lingering kidney ailment. In Toronto, she enrolled in the nurse training program offered by the nuns at St. Michael's Hospital, the only healthcare institution at the time to accept Jewish nursing students. The nuns were exacting disciplinarians and instilled in my mother a determination to do things properly and with precision. There were curfews, severe dress codes and punishments for breaking stride. After graduating, Beth practiced for two years as a surgical nurse.

When Al and Beth met, it was love at first sight. They told me this not long ago as they sat in the den in their customary places: my dad at his desk and my mom on the couch near the bookshelves.

"We had a blind date and that was it," Al shrugged. "After that, I went up north to Iroquois Falls where her parents were. We drove up and it was eight or nine hours by car. We were there for two or

My mom, Beth, and Geoff, Debbie and me (l-r) visiting Ansonville, Ont., 1962.

three days, and that is where I met my future in-laws." Al and Beth married on Sept. 22, 1953.

Their partnership has thrived over more than six decades of marriage, and included many stints when Beth would ride shotgun in their car as Al traversed Toronto's industrial subdivisions, trawling for sales leads. In those early days, she would mark down the names of companies and their addresses, and Al would cross-reference their executives' addresses when they got back to the den. I joke that Beth was Al's cold-call co-pilot—ever the skeptical pessimist who would, nonetheless, allow herself to be won over by Al's relentlessly upbeat outlook. They balanced out one another.

And still do.

From the outset of his career in the financial industry, Al had come to understand why prospective clients could be persuaded to switch brokers so readily. Long before the advent of a portfolio management fee, brokers earned a commission on each trade, and clients had little independent information about the companies whose stocks they were buying. Consequently, Al recalls, some brokers constantly had to look for new prospects because their old clients had lost all their money on risky trades, and decided to bail. "There was a lot of 'churning and burning' going on in the industry at that time as a result of everyone trading too much. They were trading too much," Al says of this earlier era. Others noticed this too, including fnancial journalists and authors such as Ivan Shaffer, who penned an insider account of the Canada's mining industry published in 1967 by McClelland & Stewart.

As he pondered the dynamic in the industry he'd chosen, Al found himself recalling what he'd learned at U of T about macroeconomic cycles, interest rates and market fluctuations. He decided to try to tailor the investment advice he gave to his clients to reflect those broader forces and figure out ways they could hedge against downturns.

Such portfolio-wide tactics were hardly standard practice in the brokerage world of the 1950s. "I realized the cycles were going to come so when things were boiling, I'd be cautious. I tried to be anti-fear and anti-greed [with my clients]." He says he did it out of an innate sense of caution, but Al also began to grasp that long-term client retention—a phrase that wouldn't enter the lexicon of business for well over a decade—was a sound business strategy in his own growing practice.

Not long after Al started building up his book of business, and with the post-Korean War market slump easing, he came across an article in the *Financial Post*. It was by Stephen Jarislowsky, the investment guru at the time who founded Jarislowsky Fraser Limited in 1955 in Montreal and went on to become an icon in Canadian financial circles. The article examined some basic principles of sustainable investing, focusing particularly on how to build a defensive portfolio that can withstand market fluctuations. The key detail was maintaining a balance, or a fixed equity ratio (FER), between stocks and income-generating investments, like

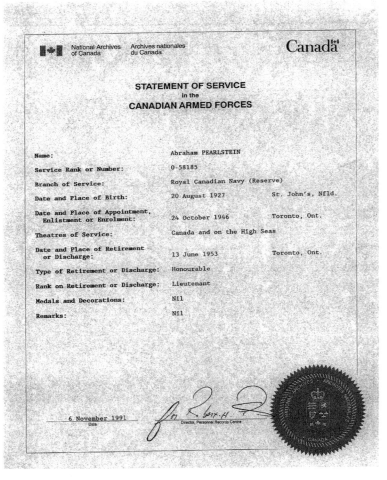

After five years in the naval reserve, Al was honourably discharged with the rank of lieutenant.

bonds or GICs, as losses in one would be offset by gains in the other.

Al found it refreshing that there was someone else who shared a similar investment philosophy to him. He told his clients that the foundation of his recommendations would be based on a simple asset allocation formula: 30 per cent of a client's holdings should be in fixed income investments, like bonds; 30 per cent in stocks; and the rest invested in more flexible ways and customized to meet every client's unique circumstances. As appropriate, Al would try to ensure that a client had enough liquidity at any given time so they could take advantage of buying opportunities. To assist clients in assessing their investment risk appetite, Al would strongly suggest they read five key books on investing.[14] After a few years in the business, Al obtained his commodity-trading license which expanded his overall view and knowledge of investment solutions that he could recommend to his clients. "People realized I wasn't a hard-sell salesman," he says. "I was different."

As he would write in the December 1987 issue of *Your Money* about the aftermath of the devastating stock market crash that year, "Since I believe that exposure to financial risk is hazardous to both your wallet and your nervous system, my approach is structured with the goal to achieve returns that are approximately two per cent to five per cent higher than the inflation rate. I regard this as the highest return you can expect without assuming an unacceptable level of risk."

---

[14]They were: *The Intelligent Investor*, Benjamin Graham (1949, Harper); *The Battle for Investment Survival*, Gerald M. Loeb (1935, John Wiley); *My Own Story*, Bernard Baruch (1957, Henry Holt); *Extraordinary Popular Delusions and the Madness of the Crowd*, Charles MacKay (1841, Richard Bentley); and *The Stock Promotion Business*, Ivan Shaffer (1967, McClelland & Stewart).

Al's investment philosophy took into consideration the underlying mathematical relationships that could either gut a client's portfolio overnight or enable it to endure for years. He also realized he had to find ways to communicate these ideas simply and quickly to prospective clients who had little sophistication when it came to investing, and likely knew nothing at all about macroeconomics or the counter-cyclical behaviour of bond yields. In short, he knew he had to find a way to sell his strategy.

In the mid-1950s, brokerage firms would often receive educational requests from the Investment Dealers Association of Canada (IDA) to send brokers to address audiences and discuss investing. Al volunteered to participate. Al soon found himself preparing to address an audience of dentists at a session to be held in a hotel ballroom in downtown Toronto. In his talk, Al meticulously laid out his case for a responsible investing strategy that takes into account everything from taxes to family responsibilities, temperament and the importance of owning a balanced list of securities that included bonds as a hedge against market downturns. He offered some tips on useful books to read and other sources of information, but warned his audience members that from an overall financial planning perspective, a holistic approach should be taken by obtaining input from professionals such as lawyers, bankers and brokers who can provide their specialized expertise.

Al finished on a note that came to define his approach, but also set him apart from many brokers. "Make a little, not lose a lot," he said. "It's amazing how hard people work at acquiring money. Yet they almost resent taking a few hours now and then to work seriously at the problem of wisely putting their money to work." He concluded with a warning: "There is no easy way to make money in the stock market."

While the speech was well received, he reckoned he needed to refine the delivery. In early 1955, he enrolled in a U of T extension university course on oral expression, offered by an expert named Helen Tucker, who offered the class to IDA speakers.

Al has saved the mimeographed course booklet and his notes, written in his tiny and precise hand, and together they offer an intriguing glimpse of a moment in time, and the thinking of a meticulous young man figuring out how he could succeed.

Al's notes from his public speaking course, 1955.

The course text begins with Tucker's statement of ideals, printed on pale blue paper and inserted at the front of the booklet. "Whatever your present environment may be," she writes, "you will fall, remain or rise with your thoughts, your vision, your ideals. You will become as small as your controlling desire; as great as your dominant inspiration." There follows page upon page of highly prescriptive information about articulation, structure and voice production, as well as lengthy vocabulary lists with correct and incorrect pronunciations. Tucker's lectures included general discussions about how to convey reputation and motivation, but also practical details such as how far one's mouth should be from a microphone.

To hear Al tell it, he soaked up Tucker's teachings. On one page of notes, he's made a list of factors that contribute to a good speech, which he's labeled "Helps": "direct eye contact, relaxation, posture, preparedness, illustration." In the next column is another list of "Hindrances"—slurring, terseness, wordiness—and also "Considerations" (i.e., "tempo, enunciation, diction"). Tucker's students had to translate all her instruction into a three-minute talk, to be delivered without notes.

Now armed with not just the content but also the communication techniques required to make an effective presentation, Al began regularly talking to audiences of prospective investors, as well as continuing with his cold calls to managers and executives at companies across the city. His days and evenings were a blur of work, and he often spent no more than 30 minutes in the office.

In the late 1950s, he plucked up his courage and went to New York over a summer long weekend to ask Gerald Loeb, the legendary Wall Street investment dealer who ran E.F. Hutton, for career advice. It was, by all accounts, an audacious gesture. Ross Knowles and Hutton had a business relationship that allowed the New York firm to acquire larger blocks of shares that traded on both the U.S. and Canadian exchanges. "Prior to going down, I prepared an outline of the questions I wanted to ask him," Al recalls. "When I got to him, the first thing he asked me was, 'Which Canadian stocks are you recommending?'"

The young man was shocked: here was one of the giants of the business, asking him for his picks. Al reeled off two names: TransCanada Pipelines and Dome Mines, which would later make thousands of investors very wealthy. Loeb then came back with the second part of his litmus test and asked if Al had read books about the stock market.

Looking back, Al realized that his interview with Loeb—an oft-quoted figure whose 1935 investing guide, "The Battle for Investment Survival," had sold hundreds of thousands of copies—would have been ended swiftly if he'd said no. But Al had read "Battle" and Loeb's question led to a one-hour conversation. "He realized that I had done some of my homework ahead of time."

By the end of the 1950s, all of Al's efforts began to pay off. His straightforward and easily understood messages about the importance of balanced investing struck a chord with people who'd seen their savings vanish. Two years after he started selling, Al began moving steadily up the company's ranking of sales performance. By 1959, at the age of 32 and just six years after that first cold call, he was ranked number one in a firm that had approximately 50 brokers.

Through successive mergers and acquisitions that saw Ross Knowles absorbed into ever larger investment firms with larger sales teams, Al continued to perform, says Brian Ayer, a long-time RBC DS branch manager who started with Ross Knowles in the mid-1960s. "We had a year-end 'Standings List' that would recognize the firm's top producer. It was almost automatic: Al was always at the top. Nobody was surprised. [He] was a perennial leader for at least 16 years."

CHAPTER 5: "A VERY RARE GUY"

At 91, Ward Pitfield, one of the Bay Street's legendary titans, looked fit and contemplative as he reclined in an armchair at the Badminton & Racquet Club of Toronto in the city's midtown, and reflected on the early days of his career on Bay Street. Though dressed casually in khakis and a blue cardigan, Pitfield's tall, angular frame and powerful handshake hinted at his once-formidable stature in the city's investment firmament—a period in the 1970s and 1980s when his company, Pitfield, Mackay, Ross & Company (PMR) boasted hundreds of salesmen, lucrative underwriting deals and a reputation for being being Canada's top brokerage.[15]

But PMR's dominant presence on Bay Street didn't just happen. The company, founded in Montreal by Pitfield's father, had to migrate its head office to Toronto in the 1960s to follow the trajectory of Canada's securities market. "It became evident that we couldn't run our business in Montreal when the major volumes were being traded on the Toronto Stock Exchange."

Reluctantly, the partners moved the firm and found themselves faced with the loss of some of its key sales staff, as well as a diminishment of the company's prominent status. "We were a major firm in Montreal," Pitfield mused, "and not a major firm in Toronto." (The B&R Club was destroyed by fire in mid-2017.)

To compensate for the short-term reduction of its retail brokerage business, PMR ramped up its corporate finance division and became active in underwriting the boom in Ontario's uranium exploration fueled, as it was, by the province's energy strategy and investment in nuclear power. As PMR sought out deals in that

---

[15]   See: http://www.thecanadianencyclopedia.ca/en/article/dominion-securities-inc/.

sector, Pitfield recalls, it kept crossing paths with the underwriters at Ross Knowles, where Al worked. "They had a pretty good corporate finance department," he said. "Knowles was looked upon as having the potential to become a power player."

By the mid-1960s, the case for a marriage between the two investment houses became glaringly obvious. Knowles' senior partners were looking to exit and PMR wanted to broaden its footprint. "The merger," Pitfield said, "was a simple decision."

After the acquisition was completed in 1967, Ward Pitfield began meeting some of Knowles' key personnel, among them the retail sales manager Ernie Pope. Pitfield describes Pope as "a guiding light," and a leading figure in Ontario's brokerage world. He oversaw a team of almost 150 stockbrokers, including a cerebral young man who, instead of picking hot stocks, spent his time figuring out what each of his clients actually needed by way of investments in order to achieve enduring returns. (PMR was acquired by Dominion Securities Inc. in 1984 and the merged firm was subsequently purchased by the Royal Bank of Canada when the federal government lifted the rule preventing banks from owning investment dealers.)

But "young Pearlstein," as Pitfield remembered Al, was well worth watching because he consistently put up the best numbers among all of PMR's sales team. Moreover, he did so with no sound-and-light show. "There was very little flash with Al. If you could get Al to say what was important to him, you'd find it pretty damned dull compared to other more gregarious salesmen. But when you went home and thought about it, you'd realize you had spoken to one of the real solid investment men." Indeed, Al soon started delivering training courses for PMR's rookie salesmen, developing teaching aids and speaking at sales meetings.

In an era before the advent of investment analysts, Al made a point of closely researching the companies whose stock he recommended and ensuring he was kept up to date on any related company news or developments that would impact his investments. He also sought to develop expertise in specialized trading sectors as a means of providing better service to his clients, although with the benefit of hindsight, the results of this added effort occasionally yielded humorous outcomes.

As an example, in the late 1960s, Al obtained a specialized broker's license because he had a client, an old friend from school, who was interested in commodities. This investor, Al recounts, sometimes wanted to buy and sell lumber contracts. On one occasion, Al, on behalf of the client, acquired 10 lumber contracts worth $160,000 that were about to expire, which meant he had to sell them quickly or face the prospect of taking delivery of hundreds of tonnes of wood sitting in a warehouse in San Francisco. With a noon deadline rapidly approaching, Al tried to contact his client, but couldn't find him. After obtaining the necessary approvals, he scrambled to find a commodity trader in New York and $200,000 in bridge financing to get those 10 contracts sold before the deadline hit. "We got the money back," Al recalls with a chuckle. "Needless to say, it was very nerve-wracking because I could have ended up on the hook. Shortly thereafter, I gave up dealing in commodities."

Such episodes, however, were few and far between and would not be tolerated under today's securities trading regulations (Al had permission back then, however). As Pitfield says now, he recognized that Al, then barely 40, was "a very rare" commodity in the fast-paced, fast-talking world of Bay Street's trading houses. "Don't think you could rebuild him," he adds, "because you couldn't."

My father and I work in a profession where it sometimes seems as if everyone wants to be known for their willingness to go against the grain, swim upstream, resist the herd mentality—pick your cliché. It is, after all, just smart marketing to position oneself as an independent thinker, an advisor not susceptible to stock market phenomena that prove either short-lived, over-hyped or simply illusory.

What strikes me, and what struck many who worked with Al, is that he actually was a person who blazed his own trail, often in the face of professional pressures to conduct business in very different ways than he did. "Al was anti-trend," observes Joan Marshall, who began as Al's assistant in 1976 and ended her career running RBC Dominion Securities' 45-person compliance division. "He would never get out right at the top or get in right at the bottom," she says. "He didn't follow the crowd."

That modus operandi included, significantly, his approach to managing his own career and the way he comported himself professionally. Al's stock holdings were very small[16] so he could be totally focused on his clients' portfolios. At the time, some brokers would get easily distracted with their personal investments. Also, in a profession infamous for long, boozy lunches with clients, Al was fastidious about having no more than one beer and, what's more, warned co-workers and protégés about the very real risks of alcoholism. "[Al would say], If you keep going to lunch with clients," recalls broker Robert Goldberg, whom Al mentored, "before you know it you're in a cycle and you're never sober."

---

[16]Al had an investment account, but he never held more than 0.5% of his liquid assets in common stock - tiny positions never recommended to clients, and Royal Bank stock he received when the bank acquired Dominion Securities Pitfield. He also owned a few senior gold common stocks worth up to 0.5% of his assets, and held as a hedge against inflation. Everything else was fixed income, mostly government guaranteed.

Nor did Al pressure his clients to buy whatever stocks had popped out of the corporate underwriting machinery on Bay Street, regardless of the company's underlying strengths. He would not rush to make any recommendations of these types of investments until he could confirm their suitability and fit for his clients' aspirations, risk tolerances and the overall composition of their portfolios. His goal was to plug holes, reduce exposure and build a kind of emotion-free portfolio that would deliver stable, year-over-year returns. "In Al's mind," Pitfield says, "it was always return of one kind or another, not specific stocks. In other words, it's not whether the stock doubles, but whether it fulfills the requirements of his investment philosophy. The individual circumstances would be different for everybody."

The portfolio-wide philosophy, which focuses on a client's longer-term financial goals, is now commonplace in today's wealth management sector. However, as Pitfield observes, "It was Al's way long before it was anyone else's."

Al, interestingly, didn't regard his approach as some kind of investment industry equivalent of a secret sauce—a formula to be jealously guarded from rivals. Just the opposite, in fact. Those who worked with Al knew he relentlessly sought to share these insights not only with his clients, but also with his colleagues, counterparts and the people he knew elsewhere in the finance world. He was famous for distributing his reading lists and serving up his steady stream of recommendations about interesting or insightful bits of news or analysis he'd come across.

For years, one Bay Street bond trader, John Braive, got a quick phone call from Al almost every morning between 7:30 and 7:45 a.m. with a morsel of advice or some useful detail that would broaden his colleague's take on the markets.

When there was more time, Al would offer a glimpse of his

ability to integrate all sorts of disparate facts and developments with his larger analysis of market cycles, interest rate fluctuations and political developments. Robert Goldberg, who would regularly go to lunch with Al, recounts what he calls a "classic Al Pearlstein devolve." "He would start with, 'Have you noticed ...' or 'Did you see this article?'" "From there," Goldberg continues, "he would devolve the entire construct behind that reference"—the complex and dynamic interweaving of macro- and microeconomic forces, market movements and politics. Armed with Al's analysis, Goldberg says, "you knew if you would be caught on- or offside." (When he began selling in the 1950s, brokerage firms had no research departments with investment analysts, so Al had gotten into the habit of doing his own meticulous evaluations of the companies in which he invested, work he often did in the evenings in our den.

Braive, CIBC Asset Management's vice-chairman (as of 2017, says Al encouraged everyone to understand the broader dynamics that influenced the behaviour of specific securities, including a recognition that the rising share price of speculative stocks may be nothing more than a temporary artifact of some aggressive selling activity (they met through Al's work advising public sector pension funds). "You've got to learn the history of the financial markets to be any good at investing," Braive says. "Al was always pushing people to become students of the market."

At the same time, Al never let himself lose sight of the fact that securities and share prices are influenced by many factors—markets, management decisions, economics, and so on. In 1968, Pitfield introduced Al to an individual who owned a private financing company that specialized in real estate—a sector he'd followed for years because so many of his clients invested in property. As Al says, "I made it my business to have some knowledge of real estate."

Al met with this individual to chat about what was happening in the economy and in the investment world. During their meeting, he mentioned in passing that a leading publicly traded real estate firm wasn't paying its bills.

"To me," Al recalls, "that was a red flag." And no wonder. That real estate firm had become something of a stock market darling in both Toronto and New York, with its share price soaring from $5 to over $100 in the late 1960s. A few weeks later, he heard another tidbit: that many of the big traders of the stock—not necessarily insiders—were using margin to the hilt. Without seeking Pitfield's permission, Al contacted the head of the Toronto Stock Exchange. He passed on his concern that another collapse may be imminent in the wake of similar meltdowns with firms like Aconic Mining, Atlantic Acceptance and Windfall Oils and Mines, and asked why the exchange wouldn't impose regulations on the borrowing of money to buy shares in these kinds of companies. "I decided that maybe I had a public duty to try and solve this before it collapsed."

What Al feared was yet another black eye for the industry. Within six months, however, U.S. securities regulators accused the company of selling unregistered stock south of the border and the TSE eventually halted trading in the stock. When the company's shares did start trading again six months later, the price had plunged by 95 per cent from its previous close.

Al had spotted the pattern early. "I wasn't trying to get a medal," he reflects. "I felt the industry had been good to me, so as a public service, I should help stop a mess."

* * *

It is very easy for me to reconcile such stories with the fundamental features of my father's personality. When my siblings and I were children, for example, we almost never saw Al become angry or lose his temper. Our mother, Beth, was mainly in charge of discipline and meting out punishments for bad behaviour. My brother and I would regularly beat the stuffing out of each other. If Al wasn't home, Beth pulled out a red dowel-like stick that was larger and heavier than a wooden spoon. "Wait until your father gets home," she'd say in a shrill tone I can still imitate. "But in the meantime, how would you like a taste of the persuader?"

If, however, we wanted to push his buttons, we all knew the one thing that would bring a sharp and irritated response. Al, as my sister Debbie recalls, had absolutely no tolerance for any sort of expressions of prejudice or disparaging remarks about anyone who happened to be less fortunate than we were. "He never said a bad word about anyone," she says.

Joan Marshall, who worked side-by-side with Al for nine years, describes him "as the most ethical stockbroker" she ever met, and further comments that Al's demeanour at work was exactly the same as it was away from the office. He was unstintingly positive and never boasted about his track record as the one of the firm's top performers.

Al liked bestowing nicknames on people. He had a habit of addressing many of his co-workers as "Sunshine," and thus ended up with that nickname, too. When phoning a client in their sixties or seventies, he'd often begin by saying, "You look great!" in order to break the ice and elicit a laugh. He also had an eccentric habit of making piercing whistling sounds if he felt the office seemed gloomy due to market losses. As my brother Geoff says, "He sounds like a weird bird."

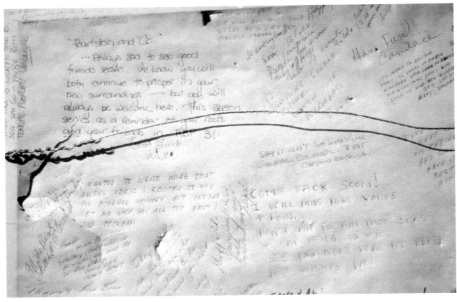

Al's nicknames inscribed by his Bay St. colleagues on the back of a framed send-off gift, 1989.

Al explains that his efforts to project an upbeat and sometimes self-deprecating persona represented his way of compensating for a naturally shy and introverted disposition—perhaps a consequence of his early illness. Al readily admits that he found selling difficult. But instead of retreating, he chose to overcome his reticence. "I tried to mask my emotions and become a little more colourful."

The outgoing persona didn't overshadow Al's determination to treat everyone with respect. Marshall offers up a telling anecdote that illustrates how he lived his principles in a corporate setting.

At one point, an older employee working in the back office at Pitfield seemed to be struggling to adapt to a new business system the firm had adopted. Some employees were grousing amongst themselves, saying this person was holding things up. But when Al heard about the complaints, he offered a gentle but firm rebuke, even though he was frequently impatient with those who would waste their time. "'Everyone works at their own pace,'" Marshall recalls Al telling those in the office who were annoyed. "He was busy and a whirling dervish, but he didn't impose it on anyone."

The portrait that emerges is one of someone who aspired to treat everyone with respect, regardless of their professional or financial status, and who also saw himself as an educator. "Whenever someone [in the office] asked me a question, no matter how busy I was I would try to help them." The reason? "When I started," he recalls, "we had these Saturday afternoon sales meetings and all these things helped me, so in essence it was payback time, and the other sales people liked that."

While Al knew from early on in his career that successful salesmen must always know how to sell themselves first, he recognized that the job turned on creating strong, positive and enduring relationships with his co-workers and, most importantly, his customers—the men and women entrusting him with their savings.

As Geoff says, "My father taught me that you have to put yourself in your client's seat."

CHAPTER 6: SWITCHING SIDES

Early in my career, I had an entry-level position in a bank, working as a commercial accounts manager. My job was to lend money, in amounts up to $1 million, to small business customers who needed operating lines of credit. The experience taught me how to quickly read and decipher balance sheets and income statements. From all those meetings with nervous prospective customers, I learned how to read the entrepreneurs who came to me for loans, and I became adept at recognizing which of their firms would likely succeed, and which would fail. These corporate clients also showed me what it was like to be a borrower and what had to be done to meet payroll.

But after five years I realized this role was not for me. I wanted something more entrepreneurial and soon left to become an investment advisor—a profession that I continue to believe is better suited for me. I now see the world through the eyes of my clients as I try to develop portfolio and financial planning strategies that will allow them to realize their dreams.

For much of the second part of his career, and indeed well into semi-retirement, Al had a similar experience. After building an exceptionally successful career as a stockbroker who would break company sales records year after year, he began consulting for the boards of several public-sector pension plans, whose trustees needed advice on how to invest the retirement funds entrusted to them.

It was, by all accounts, a highly anomalous role—a stock broker working on the so-called buy side of the business. Indeed, no one but Al had a foot in both those worlds. In today's investment world, such an arrangement would be unthinkable.

CIBC's John Braive, who was a founder of TAL Investment Counsel, worked closely with Al during this period. He says he didn't encounter investment industry people who could make that kind of change. "It's very rare for you to see this jump," he told me. "Just Al, really."

* * *

The story of Al's entry into the pension consulting business begins, interestingly enough, with a rejection. Looking back, it seems to be one of those door-closes, window-opens junctures.

In 1964, scouting around for new ways of sharing his knowledge about investing, the markets and the impact of interest rate fluctuations, Al called up Jim Gillies, then Dean of York University's business school, with an unsolicited inquiry: Could he join the faculty as a part-time lecturer? While he surely had the experiential qualifications—he'd navigated his clients by then through half a dozen cyclical downturns—Gillies told Al that he wasn't eligible because he didn't have a PhD.

At that time, investing clubs were becoming popular. Al knew a few teachers who belonged to these informal networks and were looking for ways to invest their savings. As he began considering what this trend meant, he realized that the pensions of public sector employees would likely become an increasingly important flow of investment capital. Existing public sector superannuation funds, which were typically managed by trust companies, tended to invest only in government bonds. That meant lower returns than those provided by more diversified portfolios, coupled with excessive exposure to one category of investment vehicle relative to others, such as stocks or preferred shares. "I anticipated that private investment counselors would be able to achieve better results than the normally staid banks, insurance companies and trust companies," he says. "People working for the banks or trust companies weren't putting in enough effort on investment. They hadn't done their homework."

It was an opportunity, he reckoned.

In his papers, Al has a document that itemizes how he meticulously set out to establish himself as an advisor to pension boards—in effect, an investment expert working, for a change, on the buy side of the equation. He began soliciting a pair of teachers' organizations—one of the large teachers' unions,[17] as well as a teachers' special fund with about $3 million in combined assets held by the superannuation department. In 1970, he added Physicians' Services Incorporated (PSI), a newly established doctor-sponsored pre-paid medical plan that also needed investment advice.

PSI dated back to the 1940s, when physicians contributed to a pooled health insurance fund, but it was superseded in the late 1960s when the Ontario government set up the Ontario Health Insurance Plan (OHIP). During the transition, Al recalls, about $15 million in capital remained from the original PSI fund. "There was a doctor on the investment committee who said, 'I don't know a damned thing about investing, so let's do this properly.'"

---

[17]One of Al's teacher contacts was the then-president of the Ontario Secondary School Teachers Federation Ward McAdam, a feisty union leader who fought for less crowded classrooms. In a testament to his remarkable persistence, Al continued to try to persuade McAdam, and later his successor Claude Lamoureux, to have the board retain his services for 28 years. He gave up after the provincial government set up the Ontario Teachers' Pension Plan in 1990.

One of the committee members and Al had a mutual acquaintance, and he was invited to meet with the group and lay out a plan.

Al's role was not to guide the investment decisions per se, but rather to help the doctors vet and select outside investment managers who would invest the funds. Using his connections on Bay Street, he brought in eight fund managers, including a three-year-old boutique firm called Beutel, Goodman & Company, to present proposals on how to invest that $15 million. The group, with Al's help, finally chose four of them, including Beutel. But within two years, they'd fired all but Beutel.

That assignment, Al notes, was one of the firm's first gigs as a pension fund manager and helped launch what would become one of Canada's most successful investment firms. Beutel today has $35 billion in assets under management, 90 per cent of which are owned by institutions like pension plans.

In 1975, Al, again through a mutual friend, happened to meet the head of a large public sector pension plan, which at the time had about $10 million invested with three trust companies. He could see they were facing the same issue as the doctors: the board's trustees—whose ranks included politicians as well employees—had no specific expertise in investment principles. Consequently, their pooled savings languished in underperforming trust accounts consisting mainly of government bonds. He offered to help them hire knowledgeable investment managers. "I used the same basic education that I did with my retail clients," he says.

It wasn't long before Al had been retained as a consultant to two other local public sector pension boards. Both retained his services for years; indeed, Al continued working for one of them until 2016. The results speak for themselves. In both cases, the value of their assets under management increased more than 10-fold, thanks to a steady growth in contributions and the savvy investing strategies adopted by the equity managers Al had helped these boards select.

For many years, Al regularly attended their meetings. The directors included active employees, retirees, elected officials and appointed chairs. In some cases, he would help them develop statements of investment principles and procedures. And with all his pension clients, he would ask money managers specializing in certain categories of investment products to make presentations outlining their strategies.

One was Braive, then a bond specialist at TAL, who had met Al through his work as a consultant for one public sector pension board. Al had invited Braive to

The den where Al did a lot of his thinking for both careers.

come and make his pitch. "Al," he recalls, "was wonderful in those presentations. Those guys would appreciate how he would take the time to explain what was going on. They didn't understand [terms like] yield curves."

With the money managers he'd brought in, Al would encourage them to be clear and straightforward with their explanations, Braive recounts. During their presentations, "[Al] would be really watching the room and making sure the comprehension was there in their eyes, and recognizing that it was important for those people [to grasp the strategy] because it's a future pension benefit." As with his retail clients, Al empathized with the trustees, Braive observes. "He realized that not everyone understands the terminology. He would always be saying [to me], 'Make sure you explain these things.'"

Some of the trustees, of course, did have detailed financial literacy skills and could quickly grasp the gist of Al's approach. John Cannell was a long-time government auditor and accountant who completed his 34-year career as the chief operating officer of one of the pensions Al advised. Cannell and Al worked together to create an investment statement of principles and procedures for the fund.

One of those procedures, in fact, clearly demonstrated Al's belief in taking the long view. Before Al joined in the 1980s, Cannell says, the board had a tendency to fire money managers if they turned in one or two quarters of sluggish results. "Al said, 'Don't do that. It's the long-term result you need to see.'"

He also pushed that board to reduce its exposure to fixed income investments as well as establish clear asset allocation policies for the entire fund—policies that reflected his fixed-equity ratio outlook.

Many years later, as the stock markets soared during the dot-com boom of the late 1990s, those policies would prove to be very useful. Several of that board's money managers began requesting the fund's trustees for permission to increase their holdings in Nortel which, at the time, represented over a third of the Toronto Stock Exchange's total market capitalization.

"While Nortel was shooting the lights out, some people wanted more exposure." But the board's investment policy strictly capped holdings in any one company. "We told them flat out that they couldn't exceed [the 10 per cent limit laid out in the policy]." While that restraint—a hallmark of Al's approach—meant they didn't reap the paper gains Nortel shares generated before it peaked in July 2000, Cannell points out that "we looked pretty smart" after the company began its death plunge.

But sometimes, the investment policies didn't provide a crisp roadmap through a potential crisis. During that same late 1990s boom, Al presented the board with a RBC Dominion Securities analyst's report predicting that global stock markets were poised to reach a "secular" peak, which means the culmination of a very long-term period of growth with successive bull markets. (By their nature, such turning points involve rarely seen flights of overconfidence among investors and swings in attitudes from irrational optimism to unjustified pessimism.) As the trustees studied that report, Cannell recalls, it became clear the fund's value might take a giant hit if the prediction came to pass. "The [board] had very few options."

On Al's advice, the pension board began negotiating the purchase of a series of hedging contracts that offered a measure of protection to the holdings against a major correction, while allowing the fund to generate gains up to a limit. The ensuing dot-com bust wasn't a correction of the magnitude that the analyst had predicted but Al's solution, Cannell says, provided the members with an important insurance policy against the risk of massive losses.

These complex and, at times, fraught, decisions would play out against the backdrop of boards' internal dynamics. These public sector pension boards tended to be very political. Some of the boards included outspoken union officials sitting across from appointed politicians with significant public profiles, as well as influence over contract negotiations. "You had to deal with both sides," Al recalls, adding that the elected officials tended not to be especially engaged with the work of these superannuation funds.

Without question, however, the most memorable character Al encountered while working as a pension consultant was John Markle, a long-time public sector employee who worked as a draughtsman for a government department for decades until he retired in 1989. A legendarily crusty figure, Markle served on his union's pension board for years, continuing long into his retirement.

Money managers and anyone else hoping to do business with the Metro pension board had to pass muster with Markle, and he was not an easy man to please. Braive recalls waiting to present to the board one day and watching as Markle, who he describes as "gruff," walked past him into the meeting room. "He'd give you the look up and down," Braive chuckles. "I'm the young guy dressed like Bay Street and he had a bit of a chip on his shoulder."

Markle didn't think much of the fast-talking Bay Street money managers who came before the board. "There's a lot of bullshit. 'I can do this, I can do that to make you money.'" But despite Al's long run as a stockbroker, Markle came to trust him implicitly and regard his counsel as factual and free of self-interest—someone, in short, who didn't set his radar pinging.

"He knew what he was talking about and he didn't try to gloss over anything," Markle recalled one sunny summer day in 2016 (he died in 2017, a few months before this book was published). "You'll never meet another guy like Al. He's totally honest. I know of no other way of describing him."

* * *

In 2016, at the age of 88, Al finally stepped away from his pension advisory business and entered something of a semi-retirement, working only three days a week and taking more time for himself and my mother. However, we spoke on the phone every day—Al had a long habit of making very brief calls to relay a few nuggets of information or advice—and went out to lunch frequently. Work wasn't his life, but it did represent an important part of who he was.

Going for lunch at 11:45 to avoid the North York noon hour rush. Me, Al, Geoff and my nephew Michael (l-r).

One of the things I've learned from all those lunches and conversations is that many of today's standard practices and rules were part and parcel of Al's own modus operandi when he was dealing with his customers back in the 1960s, 1970s and 1980s. Al was determined to retain clients by ensuring his service standards were always aligned to their best interests. It was a core principle, and one he sought to instill in everyone with whom he dealt.

PART II: MARK'S STORY

Much has changed in the investment industry since Al's days as one of the most respected brokers on Bay Street. The chapters that follow trace my career: how I joined Al's team in 1990 and built on my father's insights to develop a client-focused wealth management approach that is closely aligned to this era's regulatory and investment expectations.

What links our two careers is a shared philosophy about the critical importance of asset allocation, sustainable portfolios and client education, as well as the recognition that the ultimate goal of wealth management is to provide individuals and their families with the choices they need to live what I call their "peak lifestyle"—in other words, the way they want to live up until and then through retirement.

CHAPTER 7: NORTH YORK

In the middle of my third year of university, I decided I had had enough of classrooms and dropped out. I didn't really feel part of the campus experience and nothing I'd learned by then seemed to be pointing me toward my future.

Dropping out was, I realize in hindsight, an incredibly important decision. Yet it was one that sorely tested the patience of my parents, Al and Beth.

Throughout high school, I had a notion that I could go into medicine because I was good in the sciences, although the subjects I enjoyed most were English, history and geography. As university approached, Al, perhaps recalling his own educational choices, urged me to enroll in a commerce program at the University of Toronto, and so I did. I respected my father, and admired his professional choices.

In my first two years, I loved the electives where we covered broad ideas about macroeconomics, history and international relations, and the complex ways societies connect to one another. I already knew that politics and economics were joined at the hip, and what could happen when an economy cratered. One of my political science professors was married to a German woman. In a lecture hall in front of 250 undergraduates, he wept as he explained Nazi Germany and the death and destruction it had caused. I'd never seen anything like that before.

Unfortunately, U of T's commerce program was mainly designed to churn out accountants and my problem was that I really hated accounting. Bolting, therefore, seemed like my only option. Although it was my mother who verbalized her anger about my choice, I could sense from his sombre mood that Al, a man renowned for his patience and good humour, was disappointed. He had worked hard and persistently for all he'd achieved, and we were expected to follow his example. Al, after all, was the unassuming guy who would call on a prospective client for months or even years to win their business. He didn't get quitting.

I was still living at home at the time and my mother made it abundantly clear that if I quit school, I would have to find work instead of lolling around the house. Without too much effort, I hustled up a job at a shoe store in the Yorkdale Shopping Centre. Although I didn't particularly enjoy the work, I seemed to be good enough at it to warrant a promotion. Soon, I decided to try something else and landed a position selling insulation in Kitchener, Ont., and then Kingston. It was door-to-door, commission-based work, and I had no choice but to figure out how to do cold calls. (The experience wasn't entirely novel. I had had a job in high school selling wireless TV converters, often in some of the city's rougher neighbourhoods.) For Al, it brought back warm memories of his early days knocking on doors in Toronto's industrial suburbs in the 1950s. He relished the idea that I was having that experience, learning about life, as he would say, in the school of hard knocks.

A buddy and I ran "Paradise Painters" for several summers, one of many jobs I held in my teens and early twenties.

Many Mennonite families lived in my territory, on farmsteads that seemed unchanged from the 19th century. At one home, a farmer opened the door and a powerful smell wafted out of the kitchen, where his wife was hard at work. To me, their home smelled like a rendering plant but I wanted to be polite, and to make a sale, so I tried some small talk.

"What are you cooking?" I asked.

I heard—or thought I heard—her say, "porcupines." My mind reeled. I remember thinking, 'You probably need to boil them to get the quills out.' Digging my hole even deeper, I followed up,

"What do you make with porcupines?"

92

She looked at me, this know-nothing city boy standing in her kitchen. "Pork spines," she said evenly. "I'm cooking pork spines."

The farmer did ask me for a quote on my insulation product but, perhaps unsurprisingly, he didn't give me his business.

After six months, I realized I'd need to get a degree in order to move ahead with my career and so I enrolled in political science at York University, where I took fascinating courses in history and strategic studies with luminaries such as the renowned Canadian historian Jack Granatstein. After I graduated in 1982, I applied to both law school and MBA programs, and was admitted to both the University of Windsor's law school and its management faculty.

Law proved to be another academic dead-end for me. I had rented a dingy, one-bedroom apartment with awful lime green carpeting and suspiciously sticky floors. As I sat at my desk and stared at the piles of dull legal tomes, I found it impossible to imagine myself doing law for a living. I lasted three weeks.

The third time, however, proved lucky. I had deferred my acceptance to Windsor's MBA program but persuaded the administrators to let me in early. I started part-time in January 1983, and hit my academic stride, charging through and completing the program by the end of 1984. I returned to Toronto and moved in with my girlfriend, now my wife, Sharon, to write a culminating 60-page thesis about pension fund management (Al, who knew a thing or two about the way pension funds allocate assets, had introduced me to some insurance and trust company investment counselors whom I interviewed as part of my research). It was a watershed spring; I defended the paper in April 1985, started working at the bank in May and got married in June.

As is true for many young people today, the post-graduation job market held another set of tough lessons. With an MBA, I was certainly qualified to work in banking but I found the work environment too rigid. After a few years, I moved to a trust company where I was part of a large team negotiating residential and commercial mortgages for the company's underwriting division. It was 1989 and the real estate markets were going crazy, as buyers and speculators chased land deals in a kind of frenzy. The ambient greed infected my co-workers as well as my supervisor, who fired me in less than a year for not writing enough loans.

At that time, Sharon and I had been married for four years. We had two children under the age of three at home, and one income. When Al asked me to consider joining his practice as a stockbroker and investment advisor, I decided to take him up on his offer. My older brother Geoff, who is an accountant by training, had joined Al's practice five years earlier, in 1985. Al had never pushed any of us to join the family business, and at this juncture he was crystal clear about the terms and conditions—while I understood that I might eventually take on some of Al's clients, I knew going in that I had to build my own practice from scratch, just like everyone else. It was trial by fire.

Indeed, during my rookie orientation program, a trainer who knew Al decided to make an example of me as the recruits took turns introducing themselves. "This is Mark Pearlstein," he told the class. "His father is Al Pearlstein. He is a living legend in this company." Sensing I'd been put in my place in a very public way, I didn't get up. I knew I had big shoes to fill. So did everyone else.

I soon discovered that I had to learn to live by my wits, and to connect basic investment concepts to my clients' life goals—a lesson Al had figured out 40 years earlier when cold-calling prospects he'd found in the phone book.

A sense of humour helped. Early on, I spent six months pounding on doors in industrial areas, often wearing a scarf, a coat and a fedora on really cold days. One of my early clients was a guy who owned a specialized manufacturing business in an industrial complex in North York. His wife and later widow was a character. A tough, blunt, chain-smoking woman, she liked her beer and boarded horses on a 20-acre farm in Bolton well into her seventies. By the time I began dealing with her as a client, she had a serious case of cardio-pulmonary obstructive disorder (COPD), but the condition did little to slow her down. As her three adult sons knew, there was no way she was going to move off that farm and into a retirement home. Once or twice a year, I'd drive up to visit. I made the trek because we got along well and because she loved my dog Sadie, an auburn mini long-haired dachshund who would come

along for the ride. At the back of her property sat two barns and a large workshop, as well as a race-track encircling a pasture. The horses would often be out grazing in the summer when Sadie and I dropped by.

Our 4.5 kg mini long-haired dachshund Sadie has a mind of her own.

The walk alongside my client, who rode around on a small tractor and puffed away on cigarettes, despite her COPD. Sadie, in turn, barked ferociously at the impassive horses towering over her. It was funny to watch, and my client and I both laughed at the sight of Sadie's futile attempt to become a herding dog.

* * *

I'm not sure if other investment advisors would offer up a personal biography featuring an opening act strewn with false starts and more than a few underwhelming career digressions. But after almost 30 years in this profession, and having built up a very successful career, I want to share these stories because I know from personal experience that life, work and financial well-being aren't a cake walk for many people. At one point or another, most of us will find ourselves stuck or unable to save or dissatisfied with important life choices that seemed so clear … until we chose them. I believe my role in the messiness of life is to offer my clients a roadmap to financial stability and balance, and a way of thinking about their investment savings holistically. Investments, for most of us, are merely a means to an end—a comfortable retirement lifestyle, a vacation property, savings for our children's education, and so on. These are lessons I learned from Al.

It's worth saying that the professional environment in which I operate has evolved greatly since Al began as a stockbroker. Regulatory change and technology have radically altered the environment, as discount brokers dispensing automated advice have dramatically accelerated the pace of the race for profits and gain.

In my corner of this industry, investment advisors and wealth managers must adhere to a wide range of rules and professional codes of conduct that didn't exist in the 1960s. It's not just that the markets are far larger and offer investors opportunities to buy exotic financial products that weren't available two generations ago. Knowing your client ("KYC") is the foundation of our business and a long-standing regulatory requirement. As licensed registrants, we are expected to undertake the necessary due diligence to ensure that any recommendations we make are suitable and aligned to meet the client's investment needs. Like our industry and the clients we serve, the definition of "wealth management" has evolved over the years. Advisors now have the benefit of being able to have various tools and sometimes team specialists to assist them in managing their client relationships.

* * *

In the chapters to follow, I will outline the way I see the relationship between global markets, interest rates and the investment puzzle, drawing on the experiences from my practice and relating them to the way I encourage my clients to think about investments and the challenging work of saving.

The core of my investment philosophy comes from Al and our shared belief in a balanced approach to asset allocation that reflects an informed long-term outlook instead of the sort of opportunism and emotion that drives too many investment decisions.

CHAPTER 8: BOOM, BUST AND INTEREST RATES

When, as a child, I used to sit in Al's den, flipping through magazines while my father prepared himself for the coming day, I didn't know I was embarking on what amounted to an extended—lifelong, really—education in the ways of markets, interest rates and the tidal movements of economic cycles.

As his colleagues and clients well knew, Al drew heavily on his extensive reading about economics and market fluctuations. However, he also integrated all of that book-knowledge with the gritty lessons he learned first-hand as a stockbroker in the 1950s and 1960s—a choppy period marked by numerous ups and downs. He shared the lessons gleaned from weathering all those downturns with his clients and then applied them to their portfolios. Living under Al's roof, I feel I absorbed those insights almost by osmosis, although the truth is that what Al imparted to me was an abiding curiosity about economic history, finance and politics, all of which I studied in university. That learning has served me well and continues to be integrated into my investment philosophy and approach to building sustainable wealth for clients.

I have also learned to season my academic learning with the real-world lessons one soaks up in my business. I often chuckle to myself because the twinned disciplines of economics and finance both operate under the assumption that markets are populated by rational actors making rational decisions.

Yet, how do we account for fear and greed within a theory that depends on mathematics and logic? Academics toss aside a theory when it no longer works and they invent a new one. All the while, investors, who sometimes struggle to make sense of the irrational currents in the market, get burned. Indeed, the financial industry is characterized by a lack of transparency, greed and what I call "super borrowing power."[18] It's true that post-crisis reforms, like the Dodd-Frank Act and Basel III, sought to contain the forces that produce these extreme market reactions.[19] Despite those measures, central bankers, especially in the U.S., also encouraged the speculative dynamic thanks to policies such as quantitative easing that rescued some financial institutions and investment banks instead of compelling them to adjust their practices. These policies beg the question: will the bubbles just keep coming?[20]

---

[18]Leverage can amplify gains and losses in the markets either quickly or over time, depending on your financial instrument of choice. Currency, for example, can be leveraged 100:1 (or even more, if the investor closes out a position on the same day). And because currencies are intimately related to interest rates, bonds and stocks, a highly leveraged currency speculator can be aiming to capitalize on all the underlying in one bet. Leverage also refers to the amount of debt used to finance a firm's assets. Companies with significantly more debt are considered to be highly leveraged. With Lehman Brothers in the run-up to the 2008 financial crisis, the bank had leverage ratios of 30:1 to 60:1. If a company owes $60 for every $1 of equity, it has a dangerously thin cushion. And the slightest drop in underlying asset values can push the firm into bankruptcy.

[19]For further information on those reforms, please see http://www.investopedia.com/terms/d/dodd-frank-financial-regulatory-reform-bill.asp and http://www.bis.org/bcbs/basel3.htm.

[20]In a 1982 essay in the Harvard Business Review, David Mullins Jr. argues that securities markets are competitive, efficient and populated by "rational, risk-averse investors, who seek to maximize satisfaction from returns on their investments ... and demand a premium in the form of higher expected returns for the risks they assume." But, he notes, the theory is premised on the notion of frictionless markets with no distortions such as taxes or regulations. (Source: Mullins, D. (January 1982). Harvard Business Review. Does the Capital Asset Pricing Model Work? Retrieved from https://hbr.org/1982/01/does-the-capital-asset-pricing-model-work).

As with Al, my academic knowledge of economics and interest rates is stress-tested on a daily basis and never more so than in periods of volatility—those moments when it's apparent that a high-pressure bubble[21] is building up in some corner of the global economy, or when the deafening hype around some kind of investment event (Bre-X in the mid-1990s, Nortel in the early 2000s, exotic derivatives and asset-backed securities in the late 2000s) is overly distracting for my clients.

As with many people in my industry, I am often asked these days what I learned from the 2008 credit crisis (and its prequel, the implosion of Canada's $30-billion asset-backed commercial paper market in 2007). Many refer to this time in Canadian history as the single most gut-wrenching market downturn since the Great Depression.

Certainly, no one I knew had ever observed anything like the domino-like collapse of venerable investment banks in the wake of the Lehman Brothers bankruptcy, nor, in the months to come, all those global financial institution and auto-maker bailouts.

Some economists still believe in this model but a growing number have gravitated toward behavioral economics and theorists like Richard Thaler, who offers a more textured reading of markets built on the idea that the agents in any market are flawed, error-prone human beings.

[21] A market bubble occurs when the price of an asset increases well beyond its underlying value. Then, something changes—typically investor confidence—and suddenly everyone wants to sell as quickly as possible. When owners can't find buyers, they drop their prices and that dynamic accelerates, leading to a sharp market contraction and deflation.

Even those of us with formal training in economics and monetary policy had to go running back to our textbooks to figure out what then-U.S. Federal Reserve Chairman Ben Bernanke was talking about when he launched his quantitative easing policy that involved the purchase of billions of dollars of securities by the U.S. Federal Reserve as a means of kick-starting the economy.[22] Only a handful of academic and investment industry economists accurately predicted the potential crisis well before it happened and I can't say I belonged to that elite club. However, in 2005, I appeared on BNN to talk about the markets and the subject of the

Al with his golfing buddies at Donalda, 2003. Sunday evenings, after his game, we'd chat about our weekend business readings and, at that time, low interest rates.

---

[22]"Quantitative easing" refers to an unconventional monetary policy in which the central bank intervenes directly in the economy to inject liquidity and reduce interest rates to spur growth. The practice involves central banks buying bonds and other securities, but the U.S. Federal Reserve in the wake of the 2009 crisis went too far, and ended up producing a situation in which interest rates were effectively negative.

housing boom was a topic of discussion along with the more standard commentary on stocks and sectors. Interest rates were rising and 10-year U.S. treasury bonds, a crucial bellwether, had peaked in mid-2007. But housing, which had been surging in value, started to fall. Investors who had clamored for a piece of that action now faced a problem.

Al and I were closely watching housing stocks peak in 2006. One was KB Home, a U.S. homebuilder and Fortune 500 company that traded on the New York Stock Exchange. For years, the firm's stock had traded in the high teens, but investors had bid it up to the $80-range in late 2005 and early 2006.

In January 2007, Bill Gross, who used to manage one of the world's largest bond funds with over $290 billion[23] in assets under management, penned a classic analysis entitled "100 Bottles of Beer on the Wall." In it, Gross unpacked the looming housing bubble and showed how it was fueled by "innovative funny-money mortgage creation, which allowed anyone to buy a house at escalating and insupportable prices."[24] He called it. By mid-summer, two real estate hedge funds connected with large investment banks had shut their doors and the year ended with an over-exposed Citigroup slashing its dividends, a move that precipitated an 18-month-long stock plunge that gutted 90 per cent of the company's market capitalization.

Most bubbles, in my experience, come from competitive over-lending. We were in the midst of the big short, but anyone who

[23]Childs, M. (May 4, 2015). *Bloomberg*. "Pimco Total Return Loses Biggest Bond Mutual Fund Crown."

[24]Gross, W. (January 2007). Pimco. Investment Outlook; 100 Bottles of Beer on the Wall. Retrieved from https://canada.pimco.com/EN/Insights/Pages/IO%20February%202007.aspx.

called it out was dismissed as a Cassandra. As Citigroup's then-CEO Chuck Prince famously said, "As long as the music is playing, you've got to get up and dance. We're still dancing."[25] I could see a familiar pattern taking shape, but it was a bit different in the run-up to 2008. The build-up took a lot longer because the rot, as we learned later, went a lot deeper.

With the meltdown in full swing by late 2008, I was sending out quarterly newsletters to keep my clients up to date, but also making calls to reassure them. There were lots of stories in my business, however, about advisors who had chosen to avoid responding to clients panicking about the plunge.

The way I saw it, the advice I provided in such periods was a litmus test of my ability to closely read the markets and make recommendations that didn't reflect or amplify the fear that gripped investors, my clients among them. I recall the case of one couple—retired empty nesters. The husband had been in a segment of the real estate business all his working life and so he knew a thing or two about risk and market cycles. They went into the crisis in reasonably good shape; they had a clear set of investment objectives and policies and about $4 million in liquid assets, investing conservatively, with 30 per cent in stocks and 70 per cent in fixed income instruments. While they lived in Canada, I had suggested they hold U.S. dollar investments to improve their diversification. For these clients, the way through the storm was to stick with high quality stocks diversified across six to 10 sectors, within a portfolio balanced out by high quality fixed income securities.

[25]Wpcomimportuser1. (July 10, 2007). Time, Economy & Policy; Citigroup's Chuck Price wants to keep dancing, and can you really blame him? Retrieved from http://business.time.com/2007/07/10/citigroups_chuck_prince _wants/.

More generally, however, I wasn't buying much during the heart of the panic, even for clients who had liquidity and might have been able to capitalize on the opportunity. I was looking for a bottom and evidence of recovery before I started to rebalance most clients' asset mixes back to pre-crisis levels. (Some who had 30 per cent equities in their whole portfolio would have been down, on paper, to 15 per cent at the bottom, whereas another investor with 50 per cent equities would have been down 25 per cent. So, for instance, for a $100 portfolio, 50 per cent in stocks declining 50 per cent would be equivalent to 25 per cent at the worst point.)

Rather than the 60 to 65 per cent equity level going into the crisis, I had lightened up on my clients' target weightings because of all my outside reading but also because I was constantly checking in with Al and asking him to make sense of what was happening. He remembered the grinding 22-month bear market that mauled investors in 1973/74, but said this one was worse.

The market did hit bottom in March 2009, when a senior Obama administration official declared that no more banks were going to be allowed to fail. At almost the same moment, the Financial Accounting Standards Board (FASB) proposed allowing companies to use more leeway in valuing their assets under mark-to-market accounting rules. On April 2, 2009, after a 15-day public comment period and contentious testimony before the U.S. House of Representatives, FASB eased those rules to eliminate the so-called positive feedback loop that can weaken the economy. It was anticipated that these changes would significantly increase banks' statements of earnings and allow them to defer reporting losses.[26] The changes, however, affected accounting standards applicable to a broad range of derivatives, not just banks holding mortgage-backed securities.

---

[26]Mauldin, J. (July 13, 2016). Mauldin Economics. Hoisington Investment Management - Quarterly Review and Outlook, Second Quarter 2016. Retrieved from http://www.mauldineconomics.com/outsidethebox/ hoisington-investment-management-quarterly-review-and-outlook-second-q1.

Amidst all the carnage, I missed that subtle mark-to-market regulatory signal and waited for a few more quarters before venturing back into the market. [27] Some clients grumbled about the fact that I had missed an optimal buying moment and their point is not without merit. Still, as I had learned from Al, it's almost never wrong to err on the side of caution when navigating stormy seas.

* * *

In the fall of 2016, Paul, one of my clients, sent me a note that offered up a reminder about the remarkably cyclical nature of markets. "Mark," he wrote, "I see talk about a bond market bubble and I'm wondering if this is applicable to me. Again, I want to keep returns out of the equation for now. I am only interested in preservation until we decide to change course."

From my experience, less seasoned investors sometimes forget the anguish of one downturn in the headiness of the next one. But it seemed the psychological impact of 2008/09 never quite disappeared, despite several ensuing years of economic growth and a robust and sustained market recovery.

The reason may have to do with the anomalous aftermath. Interest rates remained at historic lows, which has meant a sharp expansion of household and mortgage debt in Canada as many families take advantage of cheap money to buy consumer goods and homes. At the same time, there was a lot of talk in 2016 about a bond market bubble and a Canadian housing bubble. [28]

Such talk brings questions from anxious clients and I have to offer my best analysis of what's happening. In the case of Paul, I reminded him that he owned a high quality, diversified bond

---

[27] See definition of "mark-to-market" here: http://www.investopedia.com/terms/m/marktomarket.asp.

[28] See, for example: http://globalnews.ca/news/2909453/canadas-housing-market-nears-extreme-bubble-warns-ex-lehman-brothers-trader/.

portfolio with an average term to maturity of approximately five years. His assets were generating income, which means he was taking less risk than if he'd been holding stocks, even if interest rates went up.

Stock markets generally fall when interest rates rise, but they sometimes fall when interest rates drop, as happened in the early 2000s and between 2007 and 2009. They can also fall when the sentiment changes to 'risk-off' from 'risk-on' or when consensus earnings reports disappoint. In the latter part of 2016, I advised my client, we were waiting for any one of these three scenarios. "Should rates rise, and there is not too much room for rates to rise in the next six months to a year given slowing global growth and high levels of debt on a global basis," I told him, "we are in a good position to add to equities."

I have also found, in the post-credit crisis period, that I've been asked more and more often to decipher the mysteries of the bond market, which, on a global basis, is far larger than the market for stocks in publicly traded companies. Bonds are essentially loans made to governments or corporations, that come with an obligation to repay them with interest. They can be bought and sold, but their market values stump most investors because their prices move inversely to interest rates. In addition, the yield curve—for instance, bond yields extending from overnight rates out to 30 years—sometimes moves upwards but they can also tack down when short-term interest rates jump and long-term rates go down. The yield curve, ironically, can even be flat and then swoop one way or the other, which is what happened in 2007.

When the familiar rise and fall of the economic cycle is eclipsed by complicated and inscrutable dynamics that produce periods such as the stagflation of the 1970s, it's crucial for the people in my business to have the ability to step way back, take a measure of the big patterns and crucial political developments, and then develop the investment advice accordingly. It's not just about running against the herd, as Merrill Lynch used to say in its ads. In my view, it's about really understanding the lay of the land beneath the feet of all those raging bulls.

In the case of the run-up to 2008 and its aftermath, for example, I explained to clients that global demand dropped off because growth had become temporarily and unsustainably fueled by unproductive debt. In fact, as the *Financial Times* reported in September 2016, the International Monetary Fund and World Trade Organization have kept cutting their global growth forecasts. And so, while the U.S. Federal Reserve has consistently predicted a lift-off, it hasn't really happened.

The reason is that debt deflation had to precede the kind of moderate inflation that drives growth but has almost disappeared from the economic landscape, like an endangered species. Debt deflation occurs when accrued debt must be written off against asset prices that have fallen below the value of the debt that the asset was collateralized against. Case in point: U.S. homes during the subprime debacle in the mid-to-late 2000s. For many people, their mortgages exceeded the market values of their homes. Owners just left their house keys at the bank. (Canada avoided this fate because we have different rules around lending.)

To compensate, governments have tried to inflate their way out of debt. In the U.S., for example, Washington bailed out the banks, meaning that all that stranded debt—for instance, the unpaid mortgages on abandoned homes, which had been securitized and sold to unsuspecting investors—shifted from the banks' balance sheets to the Federal Reserve's balance sheet.

Many recent independent academic studies have shown that

when debt gets to a certain level close to or above GDP[29], growth actually slows even when interest rates are low. In the U.S., the government sought to keep the public spending by expanding entitlements, such as food stamp programs. In Canada and other countries, the solution has been to boost infrastructure spending.

Did these fixes work? While in the U.S. and Canada some families' personal balance sheets did improve by the mid-2010s, others have seen a run-up in new forms of debt—student and car loans, consumer loans, second mortgages and so on. (In Canada, as of mid-2016 the debt-to-disposable-income ratio sat at 168 per cent.[30])

Solutions? It's unlikely we are going to see dramatic productivity improvements. And infrastructure investments, though a counterbalance to a sluggish economy and unemployment, can take years to produce an impact. As I surveyed the signals in the years after the global economy hit bottom in early 2009, my sense was that as of late 2016, we were facing the headwinds of middling growth at stall speed at best—and all that such developments could entail for the global economy, stocks, bonds and, ultimately, the savings of people closing in on retirement.

Take Janet, whom I met a conference. A Canadian with a busy career, Janet had just relocated from the U.S. to Toronto. She owned some American and Canadian liquid funds, but had decided to transfer most of her holdings to Canada before the market peaked in 2015. Janet's immediate dilemma: her RRSP was stuffed to the gills with speculative investments and equity-heavy mutual

---

[29]Ibid note 27.

[30]CBC News. (Posted Sept. 15, 2016). CBC News. Business. Canadian key household debt ratio hits record high. Retrieved from http://www.cbc.ca/news/business/debt-income-ratio-record-1.3763343.

funds with high MERs that would be expensive to move. Her other problem was that she was dealing with an international stockbroker and investment company that appeared, from my review of her portfolio, not to be meeting her client service expectations.

When Janet finally became a client of mine in 2015, she agreed with my recommendation to reduce her equity holdings to 60 per cent from more than 90 per cent. We sorted out some residual fee problems and a tax treatment question related to her U.S. holdings. In the end, I was able to rebalance her portfolio by 2016, adding new securities that were aligned to her risk tolerance. Given the shock waves produced by the devaluation of the Chinese yuan and then a small market correction in August 2015, I realized that dialing down her exposure had been the right thing to do.

Between 2014 and 2016, while she held this portfolio, the markets were churning and surging while interest rates had been grazing zero for years, thereby forcing investors like Janet to speculate by default.

(My professional assessment was that Janet may have failed to account for what's called recency bias, which is a tendency to believe that something is more likely to recur if it happened in the recent past or, conversely, that an event is less likely to happen again if the previous instance occurred a long time ago.)

Throughout the mid-2010s, the central banks kept rates low in the mistaken belief that they could generate growth with cheap money, despite ample academic evidence that such monetary policy tactics don't work when global debt levels are so high. The consumer credit bubble that resulted was nothing more than a substitute for falling real incomes, and the time will come when everyone has to pay the price. Indeed, this is the third time in 16 years that monetary policy authorities have created a bubble.

When will it end? My own view: when the confidence in the central banks wanes. Instead, we continue to kick the can down the road. In the absence of mindful and clear-headed advice to the contrary, ordinary investors like Janet in such a confused climate are forced to gamble. They leave themselves little protection, and insufficient liquid reserves to use when the opportunities are there for the taking.

CHAPTER 9: OUR PEAK LIFESTYLE

For many people, busy may be the defining condition of their modern life. We spend so much time preoccupied with our day-to-day activities—children, careers, health, aging parents, household tasks, vacation planning—that we don't stop to consider our longer-term futures and the key questions hovering over the horizon such as:

- What will my retirement look like?
- When will it start?
- Can I take care of all of my more immediate priorities— like setting aside enough for tuition money for the kids— while still continuing to plan for the future?
- Will I outlive my money?

Even those who've set up automatic RRSP or TFSA[31] contributions may not have thought about retirement itself. In the

---

[31] An RRSP is a tax-sheltered investment vehicle that provides individuals with an effective means of saving for retirement. Contributions to an RRSP result in a tax deduction, and the income earned in the plan compounds on a tax-deferred basis. Individuals with RRSP contribution room in Canada may contribute to an RRSP up to the end of the year in which the plan holder reaches age 71. A Registered Retirement Income Fund (RRIF), in turn, is an arrangement between an individual, the annuitant and a carrier (a financial institution authorized to offer RRSPs/RRIFs) under which payments are made to the annuitant of at least a minimum amount each year. Lastly, a Tax-Free Savings Account (TFSA) allows an individual to earn tax-free investment income, benefit from tax-free compounded growth and make tax-free withdrawals at any time. Individuals can contribute up to $5,500 annually, carry forward unused contribution room indefinitely and add any amounts withdrawn back to their available contribution room.

hurly-burly of the here-and-now, the period when such questions demand answers seems a long way off—until it's not.

When Al applied his encyclopedic knowledge of economic cycles, interest rate swings and asset allocation formulas to his clients' portfolios, he was, in effect, providing them with the potential of attaining a financially comfortable future. His philosophy of balanced portfolios that were engineered to withstand market fluctuations while growing sustainably was geared toward the goal of arriving at retirement with a properly fortified pool of savings. Al believed very strongly in ensuring clients not only met their investment objects but were also positioned to meet future retirement goals.

In my own practice, I focus on prospective clients who have amassed enough wealth to ensure a comfortable retirement. Sometimes successful entrepreneurs or savvy investors, they may bring highly specific objectives to their investing and financial planning activities—for instance, backing early-stage companies, making strategic philanthropic donations and focusing on specific sectors.

Most clients, however, are comfortable but not ultra-rich— they're professionals, business owners, retirees and those who still have several years of work-life in front of them. Most have no debt and some are looking ahead to defined benefit pension plans. The sources of their incomes vary greatly but there is a common denominator—they appreciate the value of financial and investment guidance.

Achieving a satisfying retirement requires active and mindful forward planning. It's a challenge and it takes discipline. You can consume now and pay for it later by not being ready for retirement. Alternatively, you can aim for what I describe as a peak lifestyle. We spend our working lives climbing toward a kind of symbolic summit—a place where we can relax and take stock and enjoy the fruits of our efforts, with our families and friends. Some people may want to travel, live abroad for a period of time, go back to university or spend lots of time on the golf course. Others see retirement as a time to cultivate a hobby or expand their collection of art, wine, antiques, etc.

The nature of retirement is changing as people live longer. Some people want to stop working completely by age 55, while others retire from their profession but establish a small business, or set themselves up as a part-time consultant in order to create a secondary income stream to supplement other post-retirement sources. As many of my clients have shown me over the years, the variations are boundless—provided, of course, that they have planned, saved and invested wisely.

***

In the coming chapters, I will talk about some specific strategies and case studies that focus on the more granular tactics of financial planning and balanced investing. Before I ever begin offering up specific recommendations to clients, I always urge them to slow down and spend some quality time simply imagining. Think about what you like to do, what you hope to achieve, where you want to be. Discuss these dreams or aspirations with your partner, your family members and your trusted advisors. Then, write them down.

The point is this: You have to have a target, or what's going to motivate you to get there? Once you have a fleshed-out vision of your destination, you can begin to calculate how much income you will need each month in order to get there. It's also important to say that the actual sum is less important than the quality of life you envision for yourself at that stage of your life. Someone living on an income of $5,000 a month can be just as content as another

113

person who has $10,000 a month. Everything depends on your values and lifestyle choices.

I also want to stress that the kind of forward planning you'll need to achieve your peak lifestyle isn't rocket science. It's about understanding your basic monthly costs and the cost of your goals and then methodically working backward from there. But what's crucial is to pause today and conjure up an image of what you want your specific peak lifestyle to look like, instead of procrastinating; eventually, it will be too late to plan.

Some people may put off this kind of forward planning because they feel daunted by the numbers and the calculations. After all, how can we know what things will cost, or what our expenses will be, 15 or 20 years from now?

What I try to convey to clients is that it's quite straightforward to break down what may seem like a daunting challenge into smaller, more manageable, chunks.

Consider the following simple example: imagine that one element of your peak lifestyle plan includes three, one-week trips a year, at a cost of about $10,000 each. Right now, you are able to put aside $15,000 a year for travel ($1,300 times 12 equals $15,600), but you tend not to be very disciplined when managing the rest of your monthly disposable income. But if you develop a strategy for saving an extra $1,300 each month, you will have enough for those three trips.

The question now becomes, 'How can you generate those additional dollars?' I usually present my clients with three options to consider: they can either work longer (delay retirement); they can impose extra financial discipline on themselves (reduce monthly expenses well in advance and set aside those unspent dollars); or they can change the risk tolerance of their investment portfolio (even though, as I remind them, there are no guarantees of wealth gain in any portfolio).

Those are the moving parts most of us have to work with.

When I engage people in a conversation about those three options, and in particular the question of how or whether to revisit investment risk, I introduce them to my approach to asset allocation: PRFER, or the "Pearlstein Relative Fixed Equity Ratio."[32]

Grounded in Al's insights about sustainable portfolios, PRFER is a straightforward framework that accounts for each individual's risk tolerance. The idea is simple. A portfolio can be viewed as three buckets of investment types. The first, which should account for about 30 per cent of your portfolio's value, is a safety bucket that contains bonds, GICs and savings accounts. The

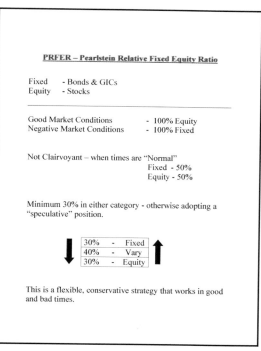

My investment and wealth planning strategy on one page.

115

principal and income are safe, but such investments are vulnerable to future inflation. The second, which should also hold about 30 per cent of your portfolio, is a growth bucket that includes equities. These investments potentially generate capital gains and dividend income and also provide partial protection against future inflation. Indeed, over long periods, equities have been shown to outperform fixed income investments by a wide margin. The safety of the fixed income holdings in bucket one and the growth potential of the stocks in bucket two work in tandem to fortify your overall investments against the ongoing volatility of market cycles.

The third bucket, representing approximately 40 per cent of your portfolio, is where we can fine-tune your investment savings to reflect your risk tolerance. How you choose to allocate that portion of your savings—I call it the vary bucket—is tied directly to your age, your investment horizon and what's going on in your life. The composition of the investments in that bucket will also reflect what's going on in the markets or the broader economy at a particular point in time. The point is that PRFER allows for flexibility—I urge my clients to revisit the mix each year—and reflects the retirement goals you've set for yourself.

These investment choices, of course, should be situated within an even wider wealth management framework that includes tax efficiency strategies, will and estate planning, life insurance and charitable giving goals.

Finally, it's crucial to remember that this whole exercise can't offer watertight assurance. Most of us, at some point, will find ourselves contending with the kinds of curveballs that life can throw our way. By undertaking the groundwork, mitigating risks in your portfolio and controlling the variables that can be managed, you will better equip yourself and your family to avoid making panicky or impulsive financial choices in the face of unexpected life changes or drastic market shifts. None of us can predict the future, but everyone can prepare and plan.

CHAPTER 10: TRANSPARENCY

When Al began selling stocks in the 1950s, broker fees were simple and everyone knew the rules of the road. Clients paid a $2.50 minimum commission per trade and the going rate was two to three per cent to buy, with the same again for a sale. On large trades, he recalls, the broker could charge a reduced commission; for example, one per cent on a $1-million purchase.

For the first two decades of his career, stock trades accounted for more than two-thirds of Al's business. But as interest rates began nosing up in the 1970s, bonds became more popular. It was his view at this time that clients were not always aware what the brokerage firms were charging for bond trades. When I joined my father's practice, I often found myself entering bond trades into the computer system and he would tell me what he wanted to charge clients, which always appeared to be in the lower end of the fee schedule

Until the 2010s, the business of fees and commissions was especially confusing and complex to some clients. Calls for reform and greater clarity go back to the mid-1990s, when OSC commissioner Glorianne Stromberg issued a report calling for major changes in the fee structure utilized by mutual fund companies, as well as the rules governing advisors who market these products.

33Source: IIROC's Client Relationship Model (CRM). http://www.iiroc.ca/news/Pages/IIROCs-Client-Relationship-Model.aspx. According to IIROC, on July 15, 2013, CRM2 amendments to National Instrument 31-103 Registration Requirements, Exemptions and Ongoing Registrant Obligations became effective. These amendments were designed to ensure investors receive compensation). Keir, K. (Oct. 12, 2016). Advisor.ca. How CSA's Sweeping Proposals Have Stolen the Limelight. Retrieved from http://www.advisor.ca/news/industry-news/how-csas-sweeping-proposals-have-stolen-the-limelight-217188? utm_source=EmailMarketing&utm_medium=email&utm_campaign=AM_ Bulletin.

While Stromberg's report led to some changes, the complexity around fees persisted. The regulatory landscape continued to evolve. In 2013, after a succession of oversight reforms over a 20-year period, the Investment Industry Regulatory Organization of Canada (IIROC) issued updated guidelines, known as the Client Relationship Model (CRM),[33] which requires investment advisors to fully disclose all of their fees to clients. The new rules came into effect between 2014 and 2016. As one industry lawyer told Advisor, "Be prepared for clients' visceral reactions when they see fee disclosure."[34]

In my practice, however, the new CRM rules were something of a non-event. For the past 15 years, I've made a point of letting my clients know precisely how much they pay me and what they are getting in return. It's a straightforward principle; after all, my role is to offer investment and financial planning advice and I believe my clients should always be able to gauge the value of my services. When I sent out a client communication highlighting the new industry CRM requirements, one client called me up and said, "Why did you send that out? I know all this." That person already knew what he was paying me.

Keeping it simple with stocks (growth) and bonds (safety), 2016.

[34]Schriver, M. (April 28, 2016) Advisor.ca. CRM2 Isn't Y2K—It's Real. Retrieved from http://www.advisor.ca/news/industry-news/crm2-isnt-y2k-its-real-204951.

Al and I have built our business on the principle that we are always transparent with our clients regarding the fees we charge and the compensation we receive. Taking this approach has led us to build long-standing client relationships that have spanned through many generations and has given us the opportunity to assist our clients through their milestones of life. We believe that client referrals are a testament to the services we provide to our clients.

In the early 2000s, when I became a Portfolio Manager, I decided to transition my business from a transaction-based commission structure to a discretionary fee-based approach. At the same time, the investment industry was also shifting and expanding its products and solutions to focus on a holistic wealth management approach. Today, the private wealth management business is the industry standard for full service investment firms like RBC Dominion Securities. The early adopters in my firm began the conversion in early 2000s. Today, the infrastructure built around this system gives RBC Dominion Securities one of the leading platforms currently available in Canada.

To make the transition, I had to overcome a considerable degree of skepticism among clients who questioned whether they'd actually be getting value by moving to a new annual fee structure, charged quarterly. My clients were right to challenge me and I knew I'd have to prove that I could continue to deliver value. So, I began pulling five years of trading data for each client. My goal was to show them precisely what they had earned on an overall return-on-equity basis and also what they'd paid me in commissions over the same period. That's how I introduced the prospect of transitioning to a portfolio management fee; I opted for maximum transparency and could then show them the benefits of a fee-based approach with real numbers. (With most clients, the result demonstrated that they were paying the same or less.)

One of the primary benefits I highlighted to my clients was that instead of seeking their approval for every trade, as a Portfolio Manager, we would create a formal structure for managing their money based on their own goals and risk tolerances.

As I worked through this transition in my practice, I never forced anyone to make the change but would always remind clients of the benefits of a fee-based and/or discretionary-managed investment solution. Many of my clients were initially resistant to making the shift, but today most see the benefits of this approach. As has been the case since I began this transition a decade ago, my clients know what they are getting from me in two ways:

- Full transparency with regard to the fees and services being provided. In keeping with the industry's regulatory requirements, all clients automatically receive performance and cost/charges reports for each of their accounts under my administration.
- A customized Investment Policy Statement (IPS) that articulates, in one place, the guiding investment strategy a client agrees to and a summary of their investor profile, which includes references to risk tolerance, time horizon, the quality of the types of securities purchased, reporting and fees. It is the road map that sets out how their accounts will be managed.

Based on the above, my clients have a clear sense of their own bottom line and are able to determine whether I'm providing them with value in exchange for those annual fees, which is exactly as it should be.

CHAPTER 11: CAUTIONARY TALES

Some people are great storytellers. Yet what I do for a living, at a very basic level, is listen to stories related to me by clients and potential clients. The narratives I hear run the gamut; from tales inflected with hope and aspiration, to confusion, conflict and uncertainty about their lives. My task is to absorb the details, ask probing questions and then distill all of the complex narratives into investment and financial planning strategies[35] that allow families to realize their dreams for the future.

It sounds simple and perhaps even formulaic, but it's not. No risk-profile investing algorithm I've ever encountered can adequately replace the hard work of understanding the individuals I meet and who almost always pose a profound question before they elect to place their trust in me: can you create a plan that will allow me to live as I wish, but not outlast my retirement savings?

* * *

Betty, a 60-year-old widow, came to meet me in my office. She seemed anxious and didn't waste any time on small talk. "Before we start, Mark," she said in a low voice, leaning forward with an expression of anxious concern, "I have to tell you something. I'm afraid I'm going to end up living on the street."

---

[35]Wealth management is a term that encompasses all things financial. *Financial planning*, a narrower service, usually means creating a strategy for accumulating wealth for retirement and personal goals. *Investment management* focuses on managing financial assets with a performance level in mind. *Wealth management* considers total net worth. Advisors in this field weigh individual financial decisions in light of an entire investment portfolio as well as other parts of the financial picture including real estate, insurance, a business and charitable gifting.

She came to me as a referral and it appeared that her portfolio didn't line up with her investment strategy and needs. But when I reviewed her monthly statements, I could see her fear of poverty was unjustified. Betty had a liquid net worth of $4 million. As she had correctly intuited, much of that wealth was balanced on a precarious mishmash of investments (she also had about $2 million tied up in real estate). Before Betty's husband Joe had passed away, the couple had come to an understanding about their financial affairs. She looked after real estate issues and household expenses, while he took charge of investing their savings.

When Joe died suddenly and Betty emerged from the shock and upheaval of that event, she turned her attention to a part of their lives with which she'd never concerned herself before. What she saw was a mostly incomprehensible list of investment holdings which included convertible debentures, silver, mutual funds, publicly traded gold companies of all shapes and sizes and shares in several oil and gas companies that had lost much of their value. Betty would characterize Joe as more of a risk taker in both life and investing. My initial view was that behind the numbers, much

My best piece of advice: it's not what you make; it's what you save and spend.

of Betty's wealth was a mess and her concerns, though overstated, were not misplaced.

Another retired couple, Phillip, 70, and Sherry, 50, shared a similar life story to that of Betty and Joe. They had purchased a lovely country home in the hills northeast of Toronto. Despite their age and lack of any sort of employment income, Phillip and Sherry—who were never my clients—had decided to carry a mortgage in order to live in this dream home. Their living expenses far exceeded what little income they had coming in. Their investment portfolio, meanwhile, consisted of $800,000 in various securities, mostly stocks. They had no pension income, which posed an immediate problem. With their mortgage coming up for renewal, their lack of income meant they'd be hard pressed to find a bank willing to give them another loan.

I could tell they were in trouble and they knew it, too. Phillip and Sherry wanted someone to tell them, in a gentle way and with realistic numbers, that they had some difficult choices to make. Indeed, when I ran the numbers for them, I had to tell them that without a substantial course correction, they would burn through their liquid assets within four or five years. Based on our discovery process, I concluded that they weren't prepared to change, and therefore I couldn't help them.

* * *

I hear stories like these every day and am humbled and honoured that these individuals entrust me to help them sort out their financial problems by developing a plan that puts them on a more sustainable path. Yet the process of rejigging or, in some cases, completely overhauling, someone's portfolio isn't just about selling off certain stocks or bonds and buying other sorts of investments in their place.

As with many complex activities in our lives, this kind of undertaking must be guided by a set of high-level principles that provide not only a framework for the investment decisions I recommend, but also a means of testing, later on, whether the specific portfolio choices we've made are meeting the goals my clients have set for themselves. Well-run small businesses do this all the time. Their owners articulate a vision of what they'd like to achieve and then set out short-, medium- and long-term goals or benchmarks to help ensure they're staying on course or making the necessary course corrections if they aren't.

Al often said that during the heyday of his career, most stockbrokers didn't spend enough time connecting their investment advice to their clients' broader financial needs. When I started as an advisor in 1990, in order to meet regulatory Know Your Client (KYC) requirements, advisors would complete forms that captured basic information about a client's knowledge of investing, certain personal details, investing horizons and a few other facts. While the format and details evolved, this KYC requirement continues to be the cornerstone of our industry.

As a professional portfolio manager, in addition to the KYC process, I am also required to establish an investment policy statement (IPS). This document brings together in one place all of the elements of a client's financial life—not just as a description, but in the form of a set of statements that translates their long-term life goals into a realizable plan. Based on my 25-plus years of experience, I have learned that much depends on an advisor's ability to listen closely to a client's stories and then apply professional judgment when devising an IPS that best fits their particular needs and circumstances.

When I initially meet with a prospective client, I'll absorb as much of their story and concerns as possible, and they will leave me with information on their current financial status, as well as an itemization of what's in all of their various regular and tax-sheltered accounts—RRSPs, RRIFs, TFSAs and so on. This is often referred to as the discovery process. My homework is to develop a draft IPS as well as two or three draft portfolios, all of it summarized in a one-page cover letter. It is my view that portfolio proposals can sometimes be dense and detailed, with lists of numbers and specific recommendations that clients may not necessarily be in a position to fully comprehend. For this reason, the personalized IPS template I use contains details such as the definitions of various financial and investment terms, asset mix alternatives, time and risk horizons, tax or other regulatory considerations and unique circumstances. In some cases, for example, a client may bring me a portfolio that includes stocks they've owned for many years and which have either some kind of special significance or a very low adjusted cost base (and therefore a potentially very large capital gain if they are sold). Some clients may have certain preferences about the way they invest. For instance, they may want to avoid tobacco stocks, or invest in environmentally responsible companies.

In addition, the IPS contains other crucial details, such as the amount of income the portfolio must generate in order to meet the client's lifestyle goals and living expenses. After all, the most beautifully constructed portfolio and IPS are meaningless if they don't address the person's day-to-day or month-to-month cash needs.

In keeping with my commitment to client transparency, the draft IPS has a specific section dedicated to the often top-of-mind issue clients want to know about, which is how I report on the performance of their portfolios and what I charge for my services. During reviews with clients, I also explain my fee as a percentage of assets and I let them know the amount that will show up on their annual statement.

During our next meeting I present my proposals in a clear and concise manner, which often leads to a robust discussion of the high-level principles that will ultimately guide the investment and planning choices, including their agreement to move forward with our working relationship.

I understand the appeal and optimism that mark these early planning exercises. A prospective client may have had a bad experience and may be reaching out to other advisors in the hopes of finding a more suitable portfolio manager. In some cases, they may have arrived at a point in their life when they've decided, for whatever reason, to be more conscientious and strategic about their financial health and wealth.

What's really important, however, is that I follow through with my service commitment to clients as it relates to accountability, transparency, and rigorous scrutiny of the investment choices I make. How do I deliver?

1. I create customized investment proposals that are aligned to the story I've heard from the client;
2. my responsive team executes the agreed investment and financial plan and provides ongoing exemplary client service; and
3. regular portfolio analysis is undertaken to ensure that portfolio holdings remain aligned to the agreed investment strategy. As additional support, my firm completes an independent risk-management assessment to ensure that my investment choices are aligned to the agreed IPS parameters.

Despite technological advances, I strongly believe that the KYC process can't be automated. I always have to make sure that my clients understand the implications of key choices and, in particular, their assessment of their own risk tolerance and understanding of the way the markets work. It's not uncommon for me to be talking to people who think they know a lot about the world of investments and want me to use some exotic new alternative asset allocation product that, they assure me, will generate home-run returns.

In those instances, it's time for me to turn the tables and relate another sort of story to such prospective clients. I'll model for them what can happen to their wealth if they over-commit themselves to a particular investment type and share with them examples of stocks that ended up tanking the way Nortel did. I will also give them a blunt assessment: if they want to be heavily invested in stocks in the hope of huge returns, they're pursuing an unrealistic goal, especially in a period of low interest rates and weak growth.

My own bottom line—rooted in my PRFER asset allocation strategy and the lessons Al taught me about sustainable investing—is simple: I am comfortable with losing a potential client who is not supportive of my investment philosophy.

CHAPTER 12: WILLS, ESTATES AND INSURANCE OR WHY THE COBBLER'S CHILDREN HAVE NO CLOTHES

My uncle, Abie Kushner, who served in the Royal Canadian Air Force, 1942.

In March 2014, I was trying unsuccessfully to reach my uncle Abie, my mom's older brother. He lived alone in Vancouver and I had been ringing him up every six weeks or so to check in. It was odd for Abie to drop off the radar like that.

Although 89 at the time, he was a highly social person who did lots of charity work. He lived independently off three pensions and, as a Depression-era child, looked after his money carefully.

Al had power of attorney for his property and I managed his investments.

When I finally tracked him down, I discovered that Abie had been in the hospital for three weeks due to a bad fall that had left him bedridden and immobilized. I asked Al to pull out his power-of-attorney documents and we quickly realized they were so specific as to be mostly useless. What's more, he had not created a power of attorney for health issues.

At the end of April, my brother Geoff and I made a high-speed emergency visit to Vancouver. We found a lawyer and brought a junior partner to the hospital to get a proper power of attorney drafted and signed. Then we raced over to Abie's apartment to find his tax documents; we took them to his accountant and got his tax return done on the spot. The whole round-trip journey took 22 hours, door to door.

Through this process, I also realized that we needed to sort out his will, or at least have a discussion about it. Did he want to make any changes or leave it as-is? I had to make sure he was satisfied with the language. Cognitively, Abie was doing fine. But some lawyers become very cautious or grow reluctant when they're asked to become involved in such discussions with the will of a very elderly and ill person.

In this case, the will review took place without any changes. It hadn't been updated since the early 2000s, which was problematic. As I knew from my practice, one's will should be reviewed every three to five years to reflect life changes, such as new children, divorce, asset growth and business succession planning. In other words, the document should mirror one's life circumstances.

Eight weeks later, Abie was suffering from severe back problems and his physicians said he wouldn't walk again. I flew back to Vancouver to clean out his apartment. I put his name on the waiting list for a nice assisted living place and fought with the hospital to prevent them from shipping him to a nursing home while we waited for a retirement home vacancy to open up. After 100 days in the hospital, Abie moved into the assisted living facility but by then, his infirmity had taken a toll on his heart. Abie died that September, shortly after his ninetieth birthday.

It took us about seven months to settle Abie's estate. The process was, all things considered, reasonably painless. His assets were relatively straightforward, as were the loose ends of his tax filings. Al, the sole executor, sweated all the finicky details with his accountant. I offered to help, but Al insisted it was his duty.

The moral is that if I hadn't gotten my uncle's papers in order at the eleventh hour, he would likely have become a ward of the state in those final months and his estate the subject of a drawn-out probate court proceeding after he passed. Such an outcome would have caused my parents much grief and regret. After all, no one wants to see a loved one's life end in a tangle of red tape and hearings.

* * *

Even at the height of his career as a stockbroker, Al and people like him tended not to concern themselves with all the adjacent elements that constitute a 360-degree approach to planning (i.e., a comprehensive analysis of savings, investment and wealth management policies; a power of attorney document; a current and properly drafted will; optimized insurance and tax planning strategies; and, in some cases, a forward-looking philanthropy plan designed to achieve individual and family goals while complementing all these other financial elements). In those days, regulations governing federal financial institutions meant that banks could only offer a select variety of insurance products i.e. travel insurance, mortgage or creditor insurance, credit card balance protection in the event of a disability, and they couldn't offer or sell insurance products. Today, while banks continue to offer these types of insurance products, investment firms have the ability to offer a broader array of insurance solutions (i.e. life, disability, critical illness, long-term care, annuities and segregated funds) to clients.

When I start a relationship with new clients, they often have well-established relationships with other professional advisors—estate lawyers, accountants, insurance advisors and so on. It is incumbent on me to work with these professionals to achieve the best results possible for our mutual client. What we've learned in recent years is that wealth planning must be seen as a highly integrated set of actions—investment choices affect tax treatments, while estate planning (for instance, the construction of a will) can point toward the use of established or newer insurance solutions that complement the balanced approach I use through my PRFER asset allocation strategy. At my firm, I am privileged to have access to a wealth management support team of professionals and experts with a wide range of resources from many providers that can further assist my clients with their planning.

As always, the ultimate goal is for the client and their trusted advisors to develop a holistic plan that is responsive and flexible, while always being focused on the best interests of the client. This journey can be complicated and at times fraught with anxiety. It often begins with a topic that most people would rather avoid: What will happen when I die?

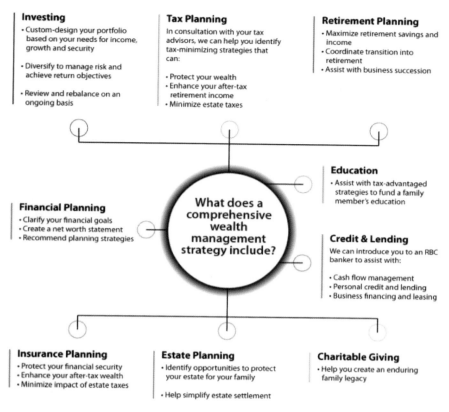

Investing
- Custom-design your portfolio based on your needs for income, growth and security
- Diversify to manage risk and achieve return objectives
- Review and rebalance on an ongoing basis

Tax Planning
In consultation with your tax advisors, we can help you identify tax-minimizing strategies that can:
- Protect your wealth
- Enhance your after-tax retirement income
- Minimize estate taxes

Retirement Planning
- Maximize retirement savings and income
- Coordinate transition into retirement
- Assist with business succession

Education
- Assist with tax-advantaged strategies to fund a family member's education

Financial Planning
- Clarify your financial goals
- Create a net worth statement
- Recommend planning strategies

What does a comprehensive wealth management strategy include?

Credit & Lending
We can introduce you to an RBC banker to assist with:
- Cash flow management
- Personal credit and lending
- Business financing and leasing

Insurance Planning
- Protect your financial security
- Enhance your after-tax wealth
- Minimize impact of estate taxes

Estate Planning
- Identify opportunities to protect your estate for your family
- Help simplify estate settlement

Charitable Giving
- Help you create an enduring family legacy

The architecture supporting PRFER, my investment and wealth planning strategy.

Wills and Estates

No one relishes the prospect of thinking about their own demise, which explains why so many adults with careers and families and assets don't have wills. Consequently, their families are exposed to all sorts of costly legal headaches and delays, should the person die. In 2012, LAWPRO, the errors and omissions insurer for Ontario's lawyers, surveyed 2,000 Canadians and found that 56 per cent of Canadian adults do not have a will and at least seven out of 10 do not have a power of attorney.

"The absence of a clear will can become a divisive and contentious issue at a time when families are already experiencing grief and can result in a range of complications, from belongings not going to the person they were intended for to court battles that cost thousands of dollars," says Raymond Leclair, the company's vice-president of public affairs.[36]

I can see these conflicts barrelling down the tracks with some of my clients, such as one particular couple in their eighties: despite their considerable wealth, their will is a DIY affair, drawn up from a template they found online. The couple has two daughters, one in Canada and the other in New York. Each will inherit a lot of money. When I advised the Canadian daughter, who is in her sixties and sometimes helps with the family's accounting, to have her parents hire an estate lawyer to review their parents' wills, she balked. I wasn't surprised. Parsimoniousness runs in that family. It was the way her willful dad ran his business for years and also how he did his books; it's unlikely any of them will change modes at this late hour. Unfortunately, the headaches, as I know from lots of past experience, will come as sure as day follows night. The lack of legal advice will take its toll in time and money, not to mention unnecessary grief and aggravation.

I tell my clients that an up-to-date will is not merely a legal blueprint for tying up loose ends. When properly prepared, it can be seen as one piece of an overall wealth management strategy. Wills can assist with optimized inter-generational wealth transfer and can potentially open the door for a range of insurance and tax mitigation strategies that provide diversification and hedging across a portfolio, and fit well into my PRFER framework for asset allocation.

---

[36] LawPRO. (May 7, 2016). Retrieved from https://www.lawpro.ca/news/pdf/Wills-POAsurvey.pdf.

Often, the first step I recommend to clients with more than $1 million to invest is a visit with a wills and estates professional. They can identify issues a client may not have considered.

Take the case of a doctor and his wife, both in their sixties, with three children and a net worth of about $6 million. His pre-tax income, which comes through his professional corporation, is about $1 million annually. When I first met them, they wanted to know if they could afford to buy a cottage for about $1 million.

When my wills and estates colleague reviewed their situation, she flagged several life insurance issues associated with their estate. I asked my insurance colleague, who is also part of my wealth management team, to take a closer look. We discovered that their previous insurance broker had failed to notify the physician about a key aspect of the policy pertaining to the renewal of an existing term insurance policy (I'll discuss insurance in greater detail in the next section). We also completed a needs analysis of their policies and identified a potential future shift in the use of funds in the account of the doctor's professional corporation.

Here's another example of why it makes sense to have a wills and estates professional vet an existing will and succession plan: I recently began working with Gabrielle, a widow with three daughters and a son, all adults with about $4 million in liquid assets. Two of her children live in the U.S. As we worked on updating my client's will, the wills and estate colleague advised her not to name her non-resident daughters as alternative executors. The reasons are subtle. A non-resident executor or trustee may be required by the court to post a security bond—an inconsistently enforced requirement that can add time and expense to administering the estate. What's more, the choice of a non-resident executor may cause an estate to be taxed as a non-resident estate, an outcome that will produce unexpected problems and costs when the balance of your planning assumes the estate is resident in Canada.[37]

All this, not surprisingly, was news to Gabrielle; the Wills and Estates Report provided her with some information she could pass on to her own lawyer. Now, her updated will contains four short paragraphs relating specifically to Gabrielle's U.S. children as beneficiaries and what happens if they predecease Gabrielle's grandchildren.

Al long ago taught me the critical importance of knowing my clients as thoroughly as possible. Practically, that means understanding not just their investments and the allocation of those holdings, but also aspects of their lives that dictate how those savings will transition from one generation to the next.

Insurance

In my experience, the wealth planning topic most people dislike talking about or reviewing as much—if not more—than wills, is insurance. While the market for insurance has become huge and diverse, few investors really understand this kind of financial product and some even have a mindset that insurance is an expense rather than a solution.

My standard explanation is that insurance should be used in a number of ways. Investors can choose from a wide range of products: sickness and disability, long-term care and many others, but they all boil down to risk planning, which is something that should inform all aspects of an individual's financial affairs.

---

[37] Having U.S. beneficiaries of a Canadian trust can also result in punitive tax treatment in the U.S. to those beneficiaries if the distributions of all income from the trust are not made annually.

While I am licensed to sell insurance, my team includes an accredited insurance specialist who assists me in finding the best solution for my clients.

The most common form of insurance is a term insurance policy, designed to replace income in the event of untimely death. While such policies represent a form of risk management for the family, term insurance as a category of investment within a broader portfolio neither grows nor contributes to an overall growth strategy.

On the other hand, permanent insurance policies (whole life or universal life) —which are essentially professionally managed investment accounts that grow over time—can be deployed tactically and offer a means of diversifying a portfolio in a tax-free way while protecting descendants from exposure to future tax bills.

Take the case of a 55-year-old client who owns some long-held real estate and business assets with low cost bases, which will generate large capital gains when they're sold or if she passes away still in possession of them. In order to offset those future taxes, she can make 10 years' worth of deposits for a whole life insurance policy. Those funds are invested in the life insurance company's diversified portfolio of stocks, bonds and real estate. Thanks to the Canadian tax code, such investments will grow without attracting taxes. This kind of hedge strategy will work even better if the contributions flow through a private holding company. The reason? Insurance proceeds can pass through something called a capital dividend account without triggering taxes. The net effect is that some of the client's funds are hived off and put into another bucket that provides equity-like returns.

In other words, for some investors, insurance solutions are an alternative asset class that provides clients with a way to diversify beyond stocks, bonds and real estate. With your deposits, you're investing in an account that grows and—the best part—is professionally managed so the client can't alter the asset mix.

Older clients who depend largely on fixed income securities should be looking at insured annuities, which are two products that work together. An annuity is a stream of guaranteed income for as long as you live. It's a simple way to turn a portion of your savings into regular income for a fixed period or for the rest of your life. And life insurance provides protection in case the recipient dies before the end of an annuity period. So for example, if someone has an annuity with a guaranteed 10-year payment period, it is possible to purchase an insurance policy that covers probate fees and pays the balance of the payments to beneficiaries on a tax-free, lump-sum basis if the policy holder dies prematurely.

Typically, if a client buys an insured annuity there is no guaranteed period, for two reasons. One, for every bell and whistle added to a standard annuity—for instance, a 10-year guaranteed period or an annuity that provides inflation protection—additional costs are incurred, which reduces the monthly guaranteed income or payout. Second, the insured annuity stays in place as long as the client lives. If a client passes away after 15 years, then the named beneficiaries receive the proceeds without having to pay probate fees because an annuity or an insured annuity is settled outside of a will.

Yes, it's tax-free. The insurance effectively insures the principal placed in the annuity. By contrast, a straight, uninsured annuity—for instance, one with a 10-year guaranteed period—is a zero-sum game. If you buy one and you pass away in five years, the remaining five years of income on the principal is paid to the named beneficiaries, end of story. The bottom line is, the insurance company wins.

However, if you buy the same straight uninsured annuity and you live until 105, you win and the insurance company loses. Of course, the insurance companies know the mortality tables upside down and inside out. They spread their risks over large population sets so they don't lose too often.

Depending on the size of available liquid assets and a client's specific requirements, only a prudent portion, about five to 20 per cent, should be placed into an insured annuity or annuity. Why? Because they are not liquid. Rather, they are contracts that can't be undone. As with everything, if you want a higher rate of return, there is a trade-off in terms of greater risk.

An alternative form of insurance is known as a segregated fund, which provides a guarantee that an individual's mutual fund assets won't lose their value in a down market. In other words, segregated funds offer insurance against the principal.

I have a client, Bill, a 75-year-old widower, but conservative investor. He found himself in the position of choosing between a segregated fund and an insured annuity. Despite his wealth, he is an anxious investor and worries about losing his savings. That's why one of his sons-in-law urged him to invest $1 million in a segregated fund with a three per cent management expense ratio (MER).

When he came in for his annual review, he asked me how segregated funds work. After explaining that they basically guarantee the capital in exchange for a fee that is higher than a typical mutual fund, I proposed an insured annuity as a better-yielding alternative to conventional fixed income products. Bill is in good health, so this product presented a good alternative for him. It was a simple solution to the sort of income needs facing an investor at that age and stage and it was also less expensive than a segregated fund. After thinking about it, Bill came to the conclusion that the segregated fund pitch he'd heard from the advisor was too good to be true. He also backed away from the insured annuity and chose an investment strategy he recognized and felt comfortable with.

In my experience, insured annuities tend to be more popular when interest rates are higher—for instance, before the 2007-09 real estate collapse in the U.S. While they are less popular now, they still get done if the pre-tax rate is attractive enough. For example, I have a client, Charlie, a retired dentist who owned a number of small, commercial storefront real estate properties prior to the debacle south of the border. He didn't want to be a landlord anymore and deal with ongoing tenant issues. He was also becoming more conservative as he got older. Charlie's portfolio included stocks and bonds. Compared to government bonds at the time, which were still paying good interest, he simply wanted a higher return but with a guarantee. Like Bill, he was insurable and in the right age bracket (65 to 75). Even after paying for the insurance portion of the insured annuity, the pre-tax income generated by it was much more attractive for him than government bonds. In this situation, everything aligned and it worked out well as a solution for Charlie.

Philanthropy and Family Foundations

Everyone knows that charitable donations of cash qualify for tax deductions. Yet I tell my clients that there are a range of more involved strategies for combining philanthropy and tax mitigation as a means of protecting wealth.

The most straightforward and popular involves donations of stock as an alternative to cash—a measure that Jean Chretien's

Liberal government passed into law in 1997.[38] Rather than giving $25,000 to a favourite charity, an investor with equity assets can donate $25,000 worth of stocks. To make this approach work best, I urge my clients to donate stocks that have a low average cost base. For instance, securities they may have owned for many years. With such securities, the capital gain is substantial and would trigger a large tax bill if liquidated when held in a non-registered account. Instead, the donation of stock effectively allows the investor to erase that future tax liability.[39]

Other clients opt to establish a family charitable foundation as the vehicle to carry out their philanthropic goals as well as minimize tax exposure and even achieve other objectives relating to estate planning. Such foundations provide families with a high level of control over the types of activities they support philanthropically, as well as a certain amount of public profile, as they become more associated with specific causes.

Such foundations can become administratively cumbersome. It's also possible that family members could lose interest in participating as the foundation passes from one generation to the next. I had an affluent client, Albert, who was a business owner

[38]The removal of the capital gains tax on gifts of listed securities began in 1997 when the Chrétien government cut the tax by 50 per cent. In the 2006 budget, Ottawa removed the remaining capital gains tax on such gifts. It has been an enormous success, as large and small charities across Canada have received more than $1 billion in gifts of stock virtually every year since 2006. Source: Letter signed by 24 leaders of national charities and nonprofits, including CAGP. (Sept. 20, 2016). How the 2017 Budget Can Help All of Canada's Charities. Retrieved from https://www.cagp-acpdp.org/sites/default/files/media/full_page_advocacy_ad_2016.pdf.

[39]According to an RBC family wealth management guide, the out-of-pocket expense on a donation of $100,000 in stocks that originally cost $40,000 is approximately $55,000. If the stocks were liquidated first, they would trigger about $15,000 in capital gains tax, so the out-of-pocket donation cost is $70,000. If a corporation makes the donation to a registered charity, it can pay the shareholders a tax-free dividend equivalent to the capital gain.

with three adult children. He had set up a family foundation but it languished after he died and the children fell into a familiar pattern of sibling conflict. Moreover, when the will was read, one child discovered that Albert, unbeknownst to him, had sequestered his considerable portion of the family wealth in a specialized trust managed by another family member. He was, perhaps not surprisingly, furious when he found out. I worked closely with one son's tax professional to sort out the financial and emotional knot Albert had bequeathed to the next generation along with his wealth. We restructured the family's finances and corporate structure to create more transparency and simplicity.

I also found a way to allow that son to take a more orderly approach to his philanthropic interests. Until then, he had made sizeable donations with little analysis or consistency—mostly acting on whatever caught his attention. Instead, I recommended that he make a one-time donation of $2 million to something called the Charitable Gift Funds Canada Foundation, which is an independent non-profit organization that allows clients to make ongoing contributions to charitable causes in a straightforward way, with the foundation handling all legal, philanthropic and gift administration tasks. A client may donate assets to the foundation, but it is set up so as to allow that individual to have some advisory rights over how the funds are invested and which charities receive donations.[40]

The benefit is three-fold: there is a tax receipt for the full market value of the donation; the capital gains tax on those securities is eliminated if the securities are publicly traded; and there is a reduction in the gross estate size by the value of the donated asset. It's a very elegant solution for wealthy individuals

---

[40]Under CRA rules, clients may contribute American and Canadian cash, publicly traded securities, mutual fund units, private shares and life insurance policies.

because it's a turnkey deal. Moreover, the fund frees clients from the continuing obligations imposed by family foundations. As Albert's son told me, his own kids weren't interested in his charitable activities and this structure allows them to be uninvolved if they want to be.

Often, with discussions about wills, estate planning, insurance and philanthropy, we find ourselves moving from the more cerebral world of investment advice to the emotional, conflict-ridden arena of family dynamics. From experience, I understand that I have to know how to properly and effectively position solutions, weigh the various interests at play and always provide options. Most of all, I need to know my clients, and know them in ways that go far beyond the columns of numbers and asset names itemized on their monthly statements. What's crucial, as I've learned from my work with older clients and their families, is that advisors and wealth managers need to have keen listening skills.

CONCLUSION

Me and Al at my nephew Michael's wedding, 2014.

In the spring of 2008, my nephew, Jared, Melissa's eldest son, decided to begin preparing for his bar mitzvah. He'd finished Jewish day school a few years earlier and had done well with his Hebrew lessons. Now, at 13, he had grown a bit rusty, so Melissa decided to hire a tutor to help him refresh. She recounts what happened next. "I said to my Dad, 'Would you like to be bar mitzvah'd?'"

While Al had been actively involved in our synagogue for many years, even serving as its president for a time, he had never undertaken this solemn rite of passage marking every Jewish child's transition to adulthood. After all, in his early teens, Al had been in Los Angeles recovering from his crippling asthma and living with relatives who weren't particularly observant. By the time he had returned to live with his parents, he was more preoccupied with university and the next phase of his life.

As it turned out, Al had considered getting a bar mitzvah alongside his oldest grandchild back in 1992. He worked with a tutor for almost four months, learning his portion phonetically because his ability to read Hebrew was limited. Al listened to tapes of his portion to get the timing, chanting and inflection right. But in the end, he called it off because the ceremony conflicted with a trip to Florida.

Now, 16 years later, Jared and Al threw themselves into the business of learning, or relearning, the Hebrew passages, some of which must be sung. Both cerebral, they were well-matched partners to take on this linguistic obstacle course.

The rehearsals proved to be a curious mix of the comic and the profound. "My dad is very tone deaf," Melissa chuckles. "You don't want to be standing beside him when he's singing." Despite his musical challenges, Al again threw himself into the rehearsal process. "He learns everything mathematically," she adds. At one point, the tutor sent her an email that said, "I've never had a student like him before."

A few weeks before the ceremony, Al and Jared, as well as Jared's parents Melissa and Stan, and Beth, all went to the synagogue to meet with the cantor and the rabbi. As they began the rehearsal, Jared realized that Al had inadvertently thrown himself into learning Jared's portion of the Torah reading! The teen had to tell his grandfather to start from scratch.

As he had before, Al re-dedicated himself to the task at hand and they reconvened a few days later, this time to go through a dress rehearsal, complete with singing. Sitting at a long table in the synagogue, Jared went first and got through his reading. When it was Al's turn, he began fumbling with his belt, loosening it completely so, as he explained to us later, he could do his breathing properly with no constraints on his muscular diaphragm.

By this point in the explanation, Melissa recalls, everyone was doubled over with laughter. The cantor, what's more, didn't miss the opportunity to throw in the punch line. "You know, Al," he said with a straight face, "when you get up there, you have to keep your belt done up." The ceremony, of course, went off without a hitch. "He got through it," Melissa says.

* * *

To participate in something like a bar mitzvah so late in life is, without question, a seminal experience, and one laden with layers of meaning. For Al, it offered a rich opportunity to close a circle by addressing a gap in his own upbringing. It allowed for expressions of spiritualism and reflection. Yet for Al, the ceremony also naturally provided an opportunity for him and his family to reflect on all the life, and the living, that had taken place up to that moment.

Looking back from the vantage point of his bar mitzvah, Al could survey what he had accomplished through self-discipline, good health, honesty and generosity. Al, as anyone who has dealt with him knows, has sought to teach and to share his wisdom. From my perspective as his son, I will say that he is blessed with a "gutte neshuma," a Yiddish phrase that means a good spirit.

In the years since this ceremony, I have had occasion to consider what Al has taught me, and also to talk to him at length about the way he set out to order and focus a life that must have seemed, early on, thwarted by the limitations of poor health and an uncertain future.

We see each other all the time at the office and, in fact, Al, Geoff, Geoff's son Michael and I frequently go out for a quick lunch to spend some time together and to clear our heads from those hectic mornings when most of the important business activity

146

takes place in our practices. Still, I wanted to understand more about what made him tick, and what aspects of his life, which had evolved so very differently from mine, had left its marks on mine. During the summer and fall of 2012, I'd drop by my parents' home and Al and I would sit down with my digital tape recorder, and he'd talk about the past. I interviewed others who knew Al, did a lot of reading, and then wrote up my thoughts and these stories. It was a period of reflection that stretched over four years.

I often came with an interviewer's agenda and questions prepared, in a list on a piece of paper. Al would reciprocate by exhuming the documents that collectively represented key signposts. High school yearbooks from his stint in Los Angeles, the notes from friends attesting to his small size and expansive intellect, an envelope of photos of Al as a robust teen on a naval adventure and the detailed, handwritten outlines of speeches he gave early in his career.

One week, we discussed his parents; the next, his bifurcated childhood and adolescence, and then his launch into the brokerage world. My dad would sit patiently, responding to my probing queries in quintessential Al Pearlstein fashion: stories meticulously constructed from the vast inventory of factual building blocks that he has always had at his disposal, even well into his eighties. These sturdy anecdotal structures he finished off with a smooth coat of his analytical varnish—ever detached and dispassionate, the logician beloved of the long view.

As I read over the transcripts of these interviews, I find the familiar tales, dutifully repeated, interspersed with his ornate explanations of market cycles and investment calls from eras that now seem impossibly remote. When I've sought to corroborate the details, a great many check out—a testament to the memory for which he was famous. On occasion, I would loop back, pressing him a second or a third time on a point where he seemed to have skated past a key detail, or a revelation that allowed the tale to hang together with greater emotional coherence.

Sometimes, Al indulged my attempts to pull back those curtains but other times, as is his right, he chose—or seemed to choose—to go so far but no further.

What rubbed off? We all ponder this problem at some point, often as our parents age and we find ourselves becoming more like them. With Al, I have a list.

He certainly spurred on my interest in economics, politics and history—the broad currents that make the world spin and work their way into the ups and downs of the markets where he and I plied our trade.

He instilled in me, somehow, a desire to be self-sufficient and meticulously well prepared. Not long ago, I found myself thinking about the hockey practices from my childhood. While my teammates loved the game and the heroics of scoring, I derived great pleasure from perfecting the practice drills my coach imposed on us. I don't remember Al ever lecturing me about obeying the coach. What I do remember, however, is watching him do his practice drills—the morning ritual of pushups, never missed, no matter how he felt. Al was always a teaching-by-doing kind of guy.

While he worked closely with many of the professional and ethical stockbrokers who built solid careers in our industry, Al didn't have patience for the bad apples who did not play by the rules and took advantage of their clients (for instance, selling worthless stocks that would eventually and inevitably crater). In his own practice, he always sought to use his extensive knowledge and learning to create sustainable wealth for his clients.

When I entered this field, in 1990, I opted to learn the business from the ground up. I was always curious about what made individual stocks and bonds move up and down, how they responded to economic and political cycles. Each one is distinctive, and that's why mutual funds are not a primary focus of my investment recommendations. I prefer to stay connected to the markets and my clients so I can continue to learn rather than relying on a third party. It's about being self-sufficient. It was how I was taught and brought up. This approach feels natural and organic.

I think Al also taught all of us the importance of stability. In his own life, he practiced the investment philosophy that he used with his clients and he wasn't much interested in the material trappings of wealth. He was an exceptionally successful stockbroker, but we lived in an ordinary home with ordinary things in it. My parents were always around. They saved instead of allowing themselves to be lured into excessive consumerism.

Al, of course, worked very hard. He retired to his den in the evenings to ready himself for the next day. Yet I wouldn't describe him as a workaholic. The work, I believe, was in the service of something more important … it allowed him to take care of his family and make sure we were provided for. As he'd often say, you have to look after yourself in order to look after others. It has become my maxim, too.

And he did look after his family, and never with a sense of merely going through the motions. Al took us to our various sports and other extracurricular activities. As a family, spent we countless hours at the Donalda Club. There were Friday Sabbath dinners and, in later years, family trips. He still calls each of us every single day, just to say something very short—a question about this or that activity, or an interesting fact.

The point is that Al made it his business to carve out that time and to create a sense of equilibrium in his own domestic world. This is hardly a surprise, given the illness and upheavals in his early years and his exile to Los Angeles. Then, upon returning, my dad went from no family to instant family. With that upbringing and his later focus on succeeding, I can see why he is the way he is.

Of course, I had no similar childhood upheavals—quite the opposite. But the practical wisdom of Al's approach and the way in which he allocated that rarest of all assets, time, is never lost on me. He modeled balance for the people in his life. And, in so doing, he gave me a better understanding of who I am. One's past, after all, is always part of one's present and serves to illuminate their path to the future. As I've learned, the only way to get there is to look forward and enjoy life's journey.

* * *

Ancestors of Abraham "Al"/"Duke" Pearlstein

Abraham (Abromas) Perelsztejn
b: Vištytis, Russian Empire
d: 1911 Vištytis, Russian Empire

Harry P. Avraham/Herz
b: 03 March 1902 Vistytis, Lithuania
d: 01 January 1993 Toronto, Ontario

David Pearlstein
b: Vistytis, Lithuania
d: Abt. 1945 Boston, Massachusetts, USA

Samuel Pearlstein
b: Vistytis, Lithuania

Yehuda Pearlstein
b: Vistytis, Lithuania
d: Vistytis, Lithuania

T. USA, "Harry1") Pearlstein
b: Bet. 1880 - 1881 Vištytis, Russian Empire
m: 1902 in Boston, Massachusetts, USA
d: 07 July 1953 Los Angeles, California, USA

Barnett Pearlstein
b: Abt. 1884 Vistytis, Lithuania
m: 28 January 1907 in Boston, Massachusetts, USA

Simchas (Simcha) Perelsztejn
b: 1882 Vištytis, Russia (today-Suwalki gubernia, Lithuania)
d: 1923 Vištytis, Suwalki gubernia, Lithuania

Philip Pearlstein
b: 1887 Vistytis, Russian Empire, now Lithuania
m: 08 June 1915 in Boston, Massachusetts, USA
d: 29 August 1958 Boston, Massachusetts, USA

Max Pearlstein
b: Vistytis, Lithuania

Louis Pearlstein
b: Unknown Vistytis, Lithuania
d: 28 September 1937 Boston, Massachusetts, USA

Golde/Goldie Rudnitsky
b: 1860 a town 35 km from Vištytis
d: June 1915 Vistytis, Lithuania

Maurice Rudner

Phillip Rudner

Abraham Pearlstein
b: 20 August 1927 St. John's, Newfoundland
m: 22 September 1953

Sister1 Rudnitsky

David Pearlstein
b: Aft. 1928 St. Johns, Newfoundland
d: 2012 Toronto, Ontario

Sister2 Rudnitsky

Sister3 Rudnitsky

Gloria Pearlstein
b: 1932 St. Johns, Newfoundland

Sister4 Rudnitsky

Shloma ?

Sarah S. Shlomo)
b: 12 September 1904 Toronto, Ontario
d: 15 August 1982 Toronto, Ontario

Four years into this project, I dropped by my parents' house one afternoon and found myself sitting with Al in his den—a space in the home that had changed very little over the years.

I wanted to pose a question that had been tugging on my sleeve, insistently.

Fifty years ago, I wondered what he thought of me wanting to be there in the den, night after night?

Al replied that he hadn't given the point much thought. He was busy and he knew I was safe and seemed content.

For many years, in fact, I used to ponder the hint of emotional disengagement in those encounters. We were physically together, but not connecting. As I grew older, I found myself searching for a more satisfying explanation, but Al is not a man given to unpacking his feelings. Instead, he lets his actions speak for him.

As we recalled those evenings, Al also reminded me about what was going on in his world. Four active children, his duties at the synagogue, his pension consulting business. What's more, he was determined not to fall victim to the bitterness that marked his own father's retirement. Al didn't want to end up like Harry.

His sense of balance, I realize, traces back not just to the lessons of his father, but also to the work and thought that took place in that den. As I drove home that evening, I found myself realizing, for the first time, that my parents had made life-altering choices in their late teens and early twenties, just as Harry had done a generation earlier in a country very far away, and just as I had done when I sought out the right career path after various false starts.

These converging currents run through the generations. We can't change who we are, but we can change how we think about the world and how we manage our own lives. That's what Al began to teach me all those years ago, in a den that I've come to regard as a kind of meridian space that links the past, the present and the future.

And what were those lessons? Looking back, I see them with great clarity, although some of them took a long time to learn.

First, you have to go beyond practical thinking and learn about yourself, read for yourself, and be yourself. And second, Al's life and teachings have served as a foundation that has allowed me to move to the next level with my family and personal relationships, and in my professional practice.

While none of this is easy, it's never too late to change how you think and how you relate to others. Everyone, after all, has a story to tell and we can choose to listen closely to those tales and soak up their relevance, or we can opt to ignore them. Finally, I have come to learn that we must take personal risks to share some of the details of our inner lives that make us vulnerable, because those stories serve to support those around us and forge stronger emotional links.

This commitment to openness and connection, in the end, is what I learned in my journey with Al.

84364221R00091

Made in the USA
Columbia, SC
15 December 2017